This Is My Beloved

MO2

G000117545

This Is My Beloved Son

Aspects of the Passion

OLIVER TREANOR

DARTON · LONGMAN + TODD

First published in 1997 by
Darton, Longman and Todd Ltd
1 Spencer Court
140–142 Wandsworth High Street
London SW18 4JJ

ISBN 0–232–52202–2

A catalogue record for this book is available from the British Library

ABBREVIATIONS

RSV   The Revised Standard Version of the Bible
JB   The Jerusalem Bible
GV   The Grail Version of the Bible

Except where otherwise stated, the Psalms are taken from *The Grail Version* and
all other scripture citations from the RSV Bible.

Designed by Sandie Boccacci
Phototypeset in 11/15pt Adobe Caslon by Intype London Ltd
Printed and bound in Great Britain by
Page Bros, Norwich

Why is human weakness slow to believe that men will one day live with God?
A much more incredible thing has already happened:
God died for men.

(St Augustine)

Contents

The Sign of the Cross

THE TENTH-CENTURY Anglo-Saxon poem 'The Dream of the Rood' – ranked among the greatest religious poetry in any language – describes a vision in which the cross itself tells of the horror of Good Friday. Even in translation it conveys a brutal earthiness that is at once so sublime, it reduces the reader to silence.

A rood was I raised up; I bore aloft the mighty King
The Lord of Heaven. I dared not stoop.
They drove dark nails into me; dire wounds are there to
    see,
The gaping gashes of malice; I did not dare retaliate.
They insulted both of us together; I was drenched in the
    blood
That streamed from the side of the Man, when He had
    set His spirit free.

High on the hill I suffered
Such grief; I saw the God of Hosts
Stretched on the rack; darkness blacker than night
Covered the radiant corpse of the Lord.
Shadows swept across the land,

Dark shapes under the low flying clouds. All creation
   wept,
Wailed for the death of the King; Christ was on the
   Cross.

(vv. 43–45)

Out of the Dark Ages comes a sensitive and sophisticated exploration of Christ's passion, emerging from a culture receptive to the reality of redemption. We imagine the Anglo-Saxons too primitive to have anything to say to us today; yet here was a society that regarded the cross not as removed from common experience, but deeply rooted in it and deeply relevant to it.

One can feel the Dreamer's sense of personal involvement in God's suffering. It comes across in the tension of the lines, the strain of the rhythm, the dark images of cosmic disruption, the heightened tone of disaster. His stream of consciousness swells to a tide of sympathy that overflows in a flood of sheer compassion. By his communion with the Crucified, this man understood pain. Moreover he found in the rood of Golgotha a symbol that made sense of affliction in terms of self-giving. Hence the poem is no tragic dirge for the death of one's liege-lord and ring-giver, but a testimony of faith in the 'Lord of Victories' who, by his sacrifice, 'has redeemed us; has given life to us, and a home in Heaven' (vv. 144–145).

How different from the culture of our time where, even in a Christian environment, we tend to avoid the crucifix directly, though its images surround us. We actually protect ourselves from the reality signified in many ways. Sometimes we do it by piety. To bow the head in reverence is one way of avoiding the wounds. Those who make the images aid and abet us.

They sand down the coarseness of the pain, clean up the blood, temper the agony on the face and limbs. Frequently they remove the corpse altogether and replace it with a risen Christ. Even the evangelists hurry over the nailing of the Messiah. Two of them relegate it to a perfect-participle clause; the other two relieve the dreadful weight of the fact by adding circumstantial details. It is almost as if the sacrilege was too enormous to deal with *en plein face*.

It is the same thing when we come to the living crucifixion of people's lives. T. S. Eliot said that mankind cannot bear too much reality. This is why we shunt the really ill into hospitals and hospices. We tell ourselves it is for their good, that here they will receive the nursing care they need. But it is also because most of us cannot handle terminal cancers, strokes, brain haemorrhages, and the like. Society does nothing to prepare us for protracted suffering. With the emphasis firmly on success and achievement, lasting pain has no part in the great plan today. Legislation on euthanasia therefore is only a matter of time. It will come in on a restricted basis at first, but will gradually extend into the whole range of agonising human situations when the public accustoms itself to the idea of death on demand.

And yet the cross of Christ is the heart and soul of Christianity. The crucifixion is the pivotal point of the gospel. It is the gospel entirely: both the historical event of Jesus on Calvary, and the continuing passion of his body, the Church. Without the protracted suffering, the harsh reality, the endless agony, the unendurable pain, there is no salvation. Remove the shadow of Golgotha and you crush hope.

This has been the Church's message from the start. As early as the first written documents of the New Testament, ministers of the word made it the hub of their preaching.

St Paul insisted to the Corinthians in AD 57 that when he evangelised them, he 'decided to know nothing among you except Jesus Christ and him crucified' (1 Cor. 2:2). As a philosophy it was madness. He admitted that. To the ears of the Greeks, pure folly; a veritable stumbling-block to Jews. 'But to those who are called . . . to us who are being saved, the word of the cross . . . is the power of God and the wisdom of God' (1 Cor. 1:18, 24).

So primal was this truth in the preaching of the apostolic missionaries, they called it *the* proclamation – in Greek, the *kerygma*. The kerygmatic proclamation was the distilled essence of the gospel. The good news in distillation was the cross. It was formulated into the briefest statement of faith for the purpose of evangelisation. Paul cited it for the Corinthians towards the end of that First Letter to remind them again of the core of their belief.

> Now I would remind you, brethren, in what terms I preached to you the gospel which you received, in which you stand, by which you are saved, if you hold it fast. . . .
>
> For I delivered to you as of first importance what I also received, that Christ died for our sins in accordance with the scriptures, that he was buried, that he was raised on the third day in accordance with the scriptures, and that he appeared. . . . (15:1–5)

Less than a quarter of a century after the event, it is already a formally fixed creed. The language in which it is presented is that of handing down, receiving and passing on. It has become tradition. Not open to the challenge of dispute, it is the basis of all further information on the life and ministry of Jesus. It provides the key to understanding the Person of Christ. Not even the resurrection – without which all faith is vain – has any meaning apart from the death that Christ endured. That death is emphasised by the burial. Both are verified by the witness of scripture. It is the bedrock of God's ultimate and definitive revelation of himself to his Church. Believe this and salvation is assured. Reject it, and sin remains, unredeemed.

That Paul had to stress the cross as faith's foundation so soon after Corinth accepted Christianity – and it was the very same with the communities of Galatia – indicates the scope of the problem historically. The language of the passion has never been easy to accept. Even today sermons are rare on the necessity of the crucifixion, let alone its good news value in respect to the coming of the kingdom. Much easier to speak about are the miracles of Jesus, his healing ministry, his moral teaching. Popular theology treats of personal fulfilment with enthusiasm, or interesting methods of prayer, or the scriptural support for environmental protection. Anything in fact that does not force us to confront the failure of Jesus as the Son of Man, and his total rejection by the world.

So what kind of Church follows a crucified Messiah? One that has received the Spirit of God. A community that rejects the cross no longer has the Spirit, even if it retains the appearance of doing so. This was Paul's great fear over Corinth. No church was so charismatic as this one, yet it stood in the gravest danger of disintegration because it was ignoring the implications of Christ's sufferings by its complacency, pride and prejudice towards its weaker members. Already the cracks were showing: factions, cliques, back-biting. While all the spiritual gifts were manifest in their midst, Paul classed them as 'unspiritual men . . . mere babes . . . men of the flesh' (1 Cor. 2:14; 3:1–3). The truly spiritual band of disciples is that which honours the death of Jesus and reproduces the mystery of it in its life-style, preaching and ministry.

Such was the primitive church in Jerusalem. In the Acts of the Apostles St Luke specifically links the descent of the Holy Spirit and the first kerygmatic proclamation of Peter. One event follows on the heels of the other as a consequence. First the mighty wind, the tongues of fire, the outpouring of the gift of speech; then immediately, Peter's Pentecost sermon:

> Men of Israel, hear these words: Jesus of Nazareth, a man attested to you by God with mighty works and wonders and signs which God did through him in your midst, . . . this Jesus, delivered up according to the definite plan and foreknowledge of God, you crucified and killed by the hands of lawless men. But God raised him up. . . .
>
> (Acts 2:22–24)

The interaction between Spirit and kerygma is a two-way process. Not only does the coming of the Paraclete lead to the preaching of the word, but where the cross is accepted the Spirit always follows in its wake. So,

> when they heard this they were cut to the heart, and said to Peter and the rest of the apostles, 'Brethren, what shall we do?' And Peter said to them, 'Repent, and be baptized . . . and you shall receive the gift of the Holy Spirit'. (Acts 2:37–38)

Thus the suffering of Jesus is never simply a past event. It is an on-going, present reality for those in whom his Spirit dwells, and who encounter him in that Spirit. St Luke's account of the resurrection appearances shows the risen Lord still bearing the wounds of his hands and feet. John's Gospel reveals the hole in his side as well. They are the emblems of love, the sign of a divine commitment that never ends. Therefore they must remain forever. To touch these wounds is to heal the wounds of disbelief. To acknowledge them openly is to release the power of the resurrection. For this death was the death of death itself. Whoever willingly bears the stigmata in his soul need never fear the second death, for he has passed over with Christ to Life.

This is the Church's vocation: to re-present and reproduce the dying of Jesus in all that it does. In the sacraments, its call to conversion, its preaching ministry, and in the life of its members. When it is faithful to its vocation it unleashes a force for good that is superior to any human power or any force of evil. That the Church has survived two millennia is proof of this. There is no earthly reason why it should have. No secular institution has a comparable record. Yet as a visible community the Church of Christ has withstood the vicissitudes of history, the sinfulness of its members, persecution, the indulgence of State protection, the downfall of empires, and the permissiveness of modern times. In each epoch it has been conformed to the sign of the cross, pierced through by spiritual or material affliction, lanced by heresy and schism, scarred in as many ways temporally as the body of its Redeemer in Palestine. But it has never failed to celebrate the cross to which it has been consigned, even though the tone of its celebration must as often be one of penitence and sorrow as of joyful thanksgiving. And that is why it has lasted. The pain of Christ's flesh is power in the Spirit, and that Spirit is the soul of Christ's body, the Church. The people that endures the passion will itself therefore endure till the end of time.

In the light of that fact, no Christian should be afraid to examine closely what is so central to his faith. St John's First Letter announces that 'perfect love casts out fear' (4:18). To look on the cross is to look on perfect love. Whoever meditates on the death of God's Son finds his fear replaced by joy. Not the kind that the world expects, but the kind – like the peace of Christ – which is beyond understanding. Such a joy transforms one's vision of everything: of one's own suffering; one's death; one's life; the world itself and one's relationship to it and to others. All this because it transforms first one's relationship to God. In Christ slain we perceive God from a new perspective. Therefore we see ourselves from a different perspective too. We begin to grasp what we mean to him, what we are in his eyes, who not only permitted but willed his Son's death to be the means and the measure of our redemption.

This is precisely what the Gospels give us: the image of God as he really is through his perfect likeness, the Beloved Son. The first achievement of the New Testament is the conversion of the imagination distorted by original sin. Instinct in fallen man is a fearsome dread of the Almighty. In Jesus that dread is converted to holy wonder and awe of God's presence – something entirely different. Adam's disobedience caused him to hide from the Lord God in the garden, ashamed of his nakedness. Jesus' obedience in Gethsemane and on Calvary permits humanity to hang naked before the Father without shame, because in the Son is revealed the fulness of the divine compassion for sinners. When we contemplate the cross through scripture, the imagination of Adam in us stands convicted of its guilty narrowness which keeps us at a distance from God. The grace of truth, flowing from the corpse of the Beloved Son, sweeps away the dykes that fear builds, and inundates the flood-plains of the mind. With St Paul we can faithfully exclaim: 'Glory be to [God] whose power, working in us, can do infinitely more than we can ask or imagine; glory be to him from generation to generation in the Church and in Christ Jesus' (Eph. 3:20–21. JB). The God of the New Testament exceeds the bounds of our expectations. The possibility of a new relationship with him is boundless too; it is infinite. The guarantee of this is the crucifixion of the incarnate Christ in whom God is not only rendered visible, but also revealed humble! It is a breath-taking revelation, especially when we consider the former distance between God and man, and then estimate the degree of love that motivated such a condescension.

Hence it is back to the Gospels that we must go, as to the source or well-spring of inspiration, if our religious imagination is to be converted, revivified, renewed. Sacred art, liturgy, pastoral preaching all tend to conflate the accounts of Jesus' passion and death. Often for very good reasons. Perhaps to present the entire scope of the event, to show its integrity by drawing on the varying details available and putting them together as a unit. Such an approach affords many lessons for meditation or counselling. However, there is a benefit to be had by examining the different perspectives on the cross adopted by the evangelists separately. That there is more than one account of Jesus' suffering is in itself significant. Why did the Church canonise four versions if one would have been enough? Perhaps each had something to offer that was worthy of attention in its own right as a specific witness to the redemption. While all four complement one another, each approaches Calvary from an angle peculiar to itself. To experience the richness of many perspectives is to appreciate better the one event. This is what we set out to do in the following chapters.

For convenience we can group the Gospel passion-narratives into three traditions: that which Mark recorded and Matthew copied with certain amendments of his own; the tradition of St Luke which is recognisably synoptic but whose tone is significantly different; and that of St John which is quite unique by comparison. All the traditions indubitably present us with the same historical Jesus, the same Christ of faith, the same total self-sacrifice, the same good news of man's peace with God, the same announcement of the kingdom. What is distinctive, however, is the personal slant of the writer on the Person of Jesus, and the particular significance attached to his death by the community from which that tradition arose in its oral form.

What also emerges from each is the hidden presence of the Father, who oversees all that takes place and directs the outcome as carefully as one who follows a secret plan. His face is never seen, yet the movement of his mind and heart towards the world is never more impressively perceptible as here, in the agonised features of his Servant and Son. On reflection, these texts dramatise the words of Jesus in the Fourth Gospel with startling credibility: 'He who has seen me, has seen the Father' (John 14:9). The shock-effect of Jesus' death shifts the entire scope of scriptural revelation on to a sphere of relevance that was incomplete until now. The raising of the cross jolts all revelation into its proper socket of intelligibility, making everything suddenly crystal clear that went before and would come after. What that revelation tells us is this: that at the heart of the universe abides an eternally youthful Father whose tenderness towards his creation is so utterly awe-inspiring, he is obliged to unveil it very slowly or it would completely consume what it had made.

Even in Jesus the ineffable majesty of love is shrouded for the same reason. Shrouded literally by the linen cloth in which he was wrapped for burial; shrouded too by the suffering of his last hours, the bruising, the swelling, the marred appearance which left him not only unrecognisable as God, but unrecognisable as man. Yet to lift that shroud with the courage of faith is to identify perfect humanity and perfect divinity. Who can identify the body of a brother and not perceive also the features of one's Father? Who can do so and not himself be changed forever? And especially after the circumstances of such a death, who could not return to his Father altered in attitude, broken in spirit, sober in grief, knowing that his sins were the cause of such terrible sacrifice?

The divinity of the Father explodes through the humanity of the Son: such is the meaning of Golgotha. Extraordinary concern for all his children on the part of the One who begets, through the abandonment of the Only-begotten. This is what the cross signifies. To read the sign by the appalling light of Good Friday is to understand the reality of both natures there – the repentant nature of the Son as man, the totally forgiving nature of the Father as God.

The christological dimension of the passion has always been clear enough. It was the second Person of the Trinity who suffered in the flesh, and not the first. The pneumatological dimension too has not been neglected: the Spirit of Jesus poured out in his last breath, flowing in the water and blood that issued from his side. But the starting-point of any dis-cussion on the crucifixion has to be God the Father since it was he who sent the Son to the cross, and to him that the Son returns, carrying with him the entire humanity that he redeemed. Often however, the Father remains a hidden Presence in the scenario of Calvary, seldom considered – as if he were not personally involved in what was happening other than in a juridical way; or thought of, perhaps, as coldly exacting his pound of flesh with calculating, inhuman justice. An apocalyptic Ancient of Days with a grudge against humanity so gross, he would accept blood sacrifice from wherever it came; like a Nazi commandant, indifferent as to which Jew he gassed in reprisal for some attempted escape from his concentration camp.

Although this idea is seldom expressed, it does lie at the base of our utter incomprehension of the mystery of Christ's death. To probe beneath the surface of the mystery is to confront a disturbing question: how could a caring Father permit his Child to suffer? Yet to see Jesus' Father as indifferent, uncaring, absent, is not only to do God an injustice; it is to misrepresent the Son as well, and to forget the Spirit who proceeds from the Father and the Son and is the bond of love that unites them. Jesus at Calvary is God's Beloved Son not despite the cross but upon it. His Father is not just a loving Father; his Father is love. In the belovedness of the one Spirit Jesus bears witness to this. But it is in the ecstasy of agony that he does so. His crucified body reveals the *shape* of the Father's love. It is cruciform: all-embracing, open, immensely patient, long-suffering. In Christ's agonised humanity that form becomes visible.

Because he is with God one God, what Christ is the Father is – they share the same divine form identically. Hence the Son is not separated from his Father on the cross. Though stripped of glory, he is not stripped of divinity. So to fail to see the Father at Calvary is to fail to recognise love in Jesus himself. It is to miss what the Father is saying through the cross, not simply in words but in the substantial act of his Word made flesh.

What God has to say is so profound, so potent, it takes him the whole of the Bible to say it. Not because he cannot find the words but because his Word is too full of meaning to be comprehended all at once; because the human ear needs time to adjust to God's dialect, his speech-form, his vernacular, his patois.

Scripturally it is a language rooted in the fortunes of fathers and sons. At the level of common parlance the context is simple enough, the vocabulary familiar, the syntax straight-forward. But gradually a sacred dimension surfaces as image and meaning converge. To those at home with the phrasing, God's fluency will not be unintelligible. It will communicate. And not just a message but a relationship. For when as communicants we receive the word as wisdom we find ourselves ear-to-Voice with a Speaker whose Mind is all compassion, whose compassion is all Presence, and whose Presence is perfect tenderness and refreshment and power.

But first we need to learn the language of love: the vocabulary, the phrasing, the grammar, the syntax, the metaphors, the forms of God's speech given to us in the Old Testament. Then we will be ready to translate into meaningful terms the complex idiom that is Calvary.

CHAPTER ONE

'My Son! My Son!'

S AINT JOHN of the Cross once made a pen and ink drawing of the crucifixion in which he viewed the figure of Christ from above. Instead of the usual one-dimensional aspect of the full vertical body: head, trunk, legs and arms as seen from ground level, what we have is a bird's-eye view of the crown and the shoulders, with the chest, thighs and feet tapering away to a point below. The arms are horizontal and close to the viewer, the nails in the hands spiking upwards on the cross-beam with uncomfortable prominence. The whole contorted body appears as if suspended between heaven and earth. Perceived slightly from the right, it makes the viewer feel almost as if he is flying down in a great swooping move-ment upon the scene which is all the more terrible because of the unusual angle from which it is approached.

It is of course intended as the heavenly Father's perspective of the death of Jesus. Fray Juan was a mystic, and had a mystic's imagination. The picture came to him during a period of contemplative prayer. Some call it a vision. But the visions of a contemplative are the product of a deep pondering on the truths of faith and their significance. What is really surprising is that no one had envisioned Calvary from such a perspective before.

Salvador Dali is one of the few who attempted it since. His famous Crucifixion, based on Juan de la Cruz, takes an aerial perspective too. This time however the artist moves towards the front of the figure so that the tapering chest and feet are pointed due south, with the extended arms rising upward and out to the east and west. Regarded from a distance the composition takes on another form, that of a bull's head, Christ's arms suggesting the horns, his dark and diminishing trunk reminiscent of the gory mouth and nose of a slaughtered animal. Strong colour highlights the dramatic impact of the spectacle, stark contrast between light and shade giving the symbolism of the image a life of its own. Implicit in the surrealist style of the work is a theology of the cross that is typical of the Letter to the Hebrews. The writer of this late New Testament document, undoubtedly a Jewish convert to Christianity, wanted to present Jesus' self-offering as the perfect antidote to sin, infinitely superior to the animal sacrifices offered for atonement in the Temple worship of the old dispensation.

> Bulls' blood and goats' blood are useless for taking away sins. . . . but now Christ has come . . . and he has entered the sanctuary (not of this created order) once and for all, taking with him not the blood of goats and bull calves, but his own blood, having won an eternal redemption for us. The blood of goats and bulls and the ashes of a heifer are sprinkled on those who have incurred defilement and they restore the holiness of their outward lives; how much more effectively the blood of Christ, who offered himself as the perfect sacrifice to God through the eternal Spirit, can purify our inner self from dead actions so that we do our service to the living God. (10:4; 9:12–14. JB)

16

The casting of Jesus as priest, victim, and both at the same time, is special to Hebrews. Not found elsewhere in the New Testament, this model, based on Old Testament thought-patterns and categories, is a distinctly Father-centred focus on Calvary. No wonder the above text should spring to mind as we look at Dali's canvas or John of the Cross's line drawing. All three bespeak a sanctified imagination that dares to think of Calvary in an unconventional way: from above rather than from below; from the mind of God instead of from the mind of man; from the purposefulness of the event as opposed to its execution; from its terminus ad quem rather than its terminus a quo. The effect is nearly mystical. It provides an inscape that immediately awakens faith to the fulness of the crucifixion as an act of God from which everything about him is laid bare to those who have eyes to see.

Without the artist – whether he be mystic or poet, painter or evangelist – such seeing would be impossible. Each in his own right is a visionary who makes visionaries of us too. We are drawn by his perspective into the current of the mystery, made participators in the powerful act of redemption. And not just intellectually. Heart as well as mind begs to be touched by what is salvific, the imagination as well as the reason, soul as well as the physical senses. The inscape of literature and art, particularly biblical literature and religious art, affects the whole stream of consciousness. It heightens feeling as much as thought and so sensitises us to the pathos of the Father-Son relationship as it unfolds before us through the crisis of pain.

That pathos is already germinally active in the Old Testament scripture which is the seed-bed, as it were, of the tree of Calvary. To reflect on the child-parent theme as presented in the early Hebrew texts therefore is to prepare ourselves for the full impact of the Jesus-Abba communion later on. This is precisely what the incarnation is about: the recognition of God in human experience, his accessibility to us in human terms. Judeo-Christian revelation is essentially sacramental in nature. It draws the transcendent God down to ground level through signs and symbols that we use ourselves, that are part of daily life; symbols and signs which are then transformed into the reality they signify.

When God became man everything became in-formed with divine significance because Christ touched everything that is proper to human being. Nothing is ordinary anymore. All things speak of Christ who himself speaks of the Father. Even that which is not proper to humanity as God made it, namely death, has been re-formed by Christ's descent into it so that death in fact is now the means *par excellence* by which the relationship between Son and Father is most explicitly opened to the world. Not just in terms of the content of faith, but in terms of our sharing in that relationship ourselves through baptism.

As the sacrificial death of a Father's Son marks the apex of Judeo-Christian revelation, so the sacrifice of a beloved child begins it. Salvation history starts when Abraham – acknowledged founder of the Hebrew nation – is tested by God's demand on the life of his offspring, Isaac. That this myth, dated about 1900 BC, should have been seized upon by the Israelites and cherished as a precious testament to their beginnings is of considerable significance. It shows that they identified themselves in terms of a relationship with God that must transcend any other, even within the family. The covenant would indeed demand supreme fidelity to the One who made them what they were.

At the same time, because of the story's happy ending (the child being spared by divine intervention), it protected the

Israelites from falling prey to the abominable Canaanite practice of child-sacrifice to which they were culturally susceptible.
God had prevented the Patriarch from killing his child – even
to prove his faith. Therefore no Hebrew had the right to harm
his little ones. It was not required within the terms of the
covenant. Indeed it was strictly forbidden. God would never
ask his people for so costly a sign of their commitment.

Abraham's faith nonetheless stood as an ideal for all to
follow, a yardstick against which to measure obedience. Its
monolithic solidity is emphasised in the Genesis text by the
emotive description of Isaac as the Patriarch's 'only son'. The
threefold repetition of the phrase (together with ten other
references to 'his son', 'your son', or 'my son') conveys the
sharpness of the sword that was plunged into the loins of
the old man's soul. 'Only son' meant not just that this was an
only child; but also that – given the man's advanced age – he
would never have another. In both senses the boy was his
father's most treasured possession.

> God tested Abraham, and said to him . . . 'Take your son,
> your only son, Isaac, whom you love, and go to the land of
> Moriah, and offer him there as a burnt offering upon one
> of the mountains which I shall tell you. . . .
>
> But the angel of the Lord called to him from heaven,
> and said . . . 'Now I know that you fear God, seeing you
> have not withheld your son, your only son, from me'. . . .
>
> And the angel of the Lord called to Abraham a second
> time from heaven, and said, 'By myself I have sworn,
> says the Lord, because you have done this, and have not
> withheld your son, your only son, I will indeed bless you,
> and I will multiply your descendants as the stars of heaven

and as the sand which is on the seashore.'

(22:1–2; 11–12; 15–17)

The deeply moving quality of the tale, both in content and style, is universal. It crosses every divide of culture or race, time or space, and makes the same impact today as then. In the third century AD, Origen of Alexandria pondered the inherent pity of the incident.

> 'Isaac said to his father Abraham, "Father".' – Spoken in that moment by his son, this word was for Abraham the voice of temptation. Imagine for yourselves how the father's heart must have been wrung when he heard the voice of the lad who was to be sacrificed! Yet, inflexible though his faith made him, he was still able to reply tenderly, 'What is it my son?' He said, 'Behold, the fire and the wood; but where is the lamb for a burnt offering?' Abraham said, 'God will provide himself the lamb for a burnt offering, my son.'
>
> This affectionate and careful reply is very moving to me.
> (*Homilies on Genesis*, Hom. 8)

Against the backdrop of this tender tale and its 'only son' motif, the New Testament comes as a shocking revelation. 'God so loved the world that he gave his only Son, that whoever believes in him should not perish but have eternal life' (John 3:16). Or as St Paul put it, even more pointedly, '[God] did not spare his own Son but gave him up for us all' (Rom. 8:32). In other words what Abraham was spared from carrying out at the eleventh hour, God did not spare himself from in the fulness of time. Such was the faith he placed in the world for love of which no Personal sacrifice was too great.

Although 'the world' in the Fourth Gospel is sometimes a

synonym for human sinfulness it can also mean the cosmos God created and filled with his own image. It is the latter sense that is intended here. For while the creation has been alienated from God by man's evil, it is still the object of a compassion so infinite that it would take the immolation of an Only Son to define it adequately.

How better could such infinite truth be grasped by mere mortals than by appealing to the natural love between parents and children? Origen (who lost his father in the Christian persecution under Septimus Severus) weighed the measure of that truth by contrasting the Old and New Testament texts.

> 'He did not spare his own Son, but gave him up for us all'. See how magnificent is the generosity with which God competes with men! Abraham offered to God his mortal son who was not to die; God delivered his immortal Son, for all mankind. (Homily 8)

The juxtaposition allows the reader to see in Abraham's courageous love for God something of God's immeasurable love for the world. The details of the Old Testament narrative intensify the comparison without losing the contrast between the two fathers and their respective sons.

Thus Isaac's journey to Moriah foreshadows the *Via dolorosa* for Origen. The wood of the burnt offering is laid upon the Patriarch's son just as the cross would be laid on God's. The boy walks beside his father, equal to him in priestly status; so Christ as God's equal is both priest and victim to his Father's will. Even the ram substituted for Abraham's child is seen as a type of God's Child, crucified as a substitute for all the sons of men.

Throughout the reader is led to recognise in the grief of Abraham whom he can see, the hidden empathy of the Father

21

whom he cannot. By observing the similarities in the two situations and emphasising the pathos of the first, the writer manages to suggest the indescribable mercy of the Almighty to mankind. It is a daring literary technique that reflects the anthropomorphic style of the Bible itself: the tracing of facial contours on the invisible face of the Divine to humanise his compassionate regard for his creature.

To read the Genesis story in this way is of course to go beyond the literal meaning intended by its author. Writing almost a thousand years before the Jesus of history, he could not have anticipated the Gospel accounts of Christ's death. He had no powers of perception above the ordinary as he committed to papyrus the oral traditions of his people. Even if his religious sensitivity to the things of God made him receptive to inspiration, it did not endow him with special knowledge of the future. In this he was as restricted as his contemporaries by the limitations of the time and place in which he lived.

What Origen looked for in this passage however was the *spiritual* meaning of the narrative – what is sometimes called the mystical sense. He wished to discover what was in the mind of its true author, God himself. No passage of scripture stands in isolation. It is understood in the context of the book in which it occurs, just as no book yields its full significance outside the context of the Bible as a whole. This is particularly so in the relationship between the Old and New Testaments. As Pius XII pointed out in his directive to scripture scholars in our time:

> What was said and done in the Old Testament . . . pre-
> figured in a spiritual way those [things] that were to come
> under the new dispensation of grace. Wherefore the

exegete, just as he must search out and expound the literal meaning of the words intended and expressed by the sacred writer, so also he must do likewise for the spiritual sense, provided it is clearly intended by God. For God alone could have known this spiritual meaning and could have revealed it to us. (*Divino Afflante Spiritu*, nn. 26–27)

In the light of this, the Abraham saga communicates truth not so much as an individual story of God's promise to one man, but as an italicised episode in a whole history of Promise and Fulfilment. Only when that history is completed in the New Testament event of Jesus does the literal meaning of all that was told before disclose its spiritual significance. Thus while the seminal, mystical sense of the father-son sacrifice in Genesis could not have been clear to the Elohist writer it was certainly clear to the One who inspired it, and became clear to the early Christians who re-read it against the full revelation of Calvary.

What is given in the Old Testament therefore is no crude foretelling of the future, but a preparation for it. So when the reader comes to these stories, bringing to them the full range of his human sensibility, he will find he is no stranger to their meaning. Catching a sense of the reality that great literature embodies and that has a life of its own, he recognises a quality of truthfulness that breaks out of the text and is beyond the control of its human author. What he reads will verify what he already knows if he has thought about life: the existence of an ultimate reality that enables him to respond to his need for God, helps him define what he means by God, and teaches him how to interpret himself. The texts of sacred scripture confront him with figures both of his own reality and of the unique mystery where God and man are connected insepar-

23

ably. These figures find their matrix in his total awareness of God's presence and plan at work in every aspect of his existence, secular and religious. Such knowing is guided by God himself. He makes clear what his purpose is and affirms the inner cohesion of his plan in its various parts as they appear in scripture and in the human consciousness. Perceived in their entirety these point to a web of love that undergirds the whole of history and all of creation and is particularly part of personal relationships, and personal sacrifice.

Because this ultimate reality lies at the base of consciousness and is not directly accessible, it requires the medium of the word to give it its expression. Enfleshed in language, it reveals at once its universal nature and integrity: what is true in the idiom of the Bible is re-affirmed in the movement of the responsive heart. As the disciples on the way to Emmaus discovered that first Easter evening – 'They said to each other, "Did not our hearts burn within us while he talked to us on the road, while he opened to us the scriptures?"' (Luke 24:32)

What is this ultimate reality which impinges on the universal experience of truth throughout the cosmos and down the ages? That the highest form of love is threefold: to sacrifice one's son, to sacrifice one's self, and to do so in a spirit of forgiveness. This God did. As Father, he gave us Christ; as Son, he gave himself on the cross; as Spirit, he ensured the entirely redemptive nature of the act by the outpouring of divine mercy through the crime committed. The cross therefore stands as *the* proto truth-event. It encapsulates all truth. All truth emanates from it directly because, as the corporate act of the three divine Persons, it marks the unique epiphany of perfect love which is diffused throughout the very fabric of existence and man's experience of it.

When, therefore, in the scriptural stream of revelation a

theme surfaces that offers a glimpse into the nature of salvation, something emerges in the text of the fulness of
meaning that God intended. The effect is to move the heart
of the sinner first to holy hope, then to the repentance that
love evokes, and finally to saving faith. To re-locate Genesis
and read it as a prelude to the gospel is to watch God carefully
preparing the human spirit through shadows in the stream for
the reality that reaches its definitive expression in Christ.

That the Abraham story is not an end in itself, that it does
not deliver the fulness of its own spiritual sense, is implied in
the name of the mountain where the tale takes place: Moriah,
which means 'God will provide'. It testifies to the character of
God's paternity. He is *the* Provider; he will always provide
what is needed. The provision of the ram in lieu of Isaac
does not exhaust his beneficence. It simply points to a fuller
manifestation of his bounty. Since it is the Infinite One who
claims the title 'Provider', nothing short of infinite provision
is worthy of the faith-expectation due to him. 'Abraham said,
"God will provide himself the lamb"' (Gen. 22:8). In terms of
the covenant, only a lamb that could justify a history of iniquity
would do for a sin-offering. For what oblation could a species
make to redress its ingratitude to him who made it? None,
because though the human race had power to offend the
Almighty, it did not have the means to expiate the offence.
The distance between creature and Creator was too vast. And
yet, in justice, only man may atone for man's crimes. An
impossible dilemma: to have incurred a debt against One so
holy that no man was holy enough to obliterate it, even though
no one but man could be held liable. Could the Provider
provide against the impossible? Yes he could: one solution
recommended itself, and so God himself became man! Origen

was right – Abraham's hope at Moriah could never be interpreted too literally, nor too spiritually.

Because justice required that a man should redeem man by making satisfaction for sin, the incarnation and Calvary are a *necessary* truth. Truth is revealed through necessity: human need calls down truth to its side. Since God's love of the truth is one with his love of justice, the crucifixion was always inevitable. But who can grasp God's love of justice and truth? Only a lesser figure such as Abraham can accommodate our limited perception of the greater reality of which Abraham and Isaac are the type. Therefore the Abraham story is as necessary as it is true. Not in the historical sense, but in the theological. It is necessary in that it calls forth our faith, and true insofar as it supplies a reason, a justification for faith by revealing the dependability of God's all-providing love. This is why the gigantic presence of Abraham overshadows the entire New Testament: in Mary's Magnificat; John the Baptist's tirade against the Pharisees; the Johannine discourses of Jesus to the Jews; St Paul's teaching on faith in Galatians; the pastorally encouraging Letter to the Hebrews. Those who opposed Christ and rejected the gospel called themselves children of Abraham; yet they failed to believe as he did because they had locked themselves into the narrower, literal meaning of the old dispensation, never progressing on to the spiritual fulfilment that its mystical significance meant them to reach. For those who did listen to Jesus, Abraham not only typified God's self-sacrificing love in offering his only son; he first embodied the obedient faith of God's true Israel, the faith that in itself justifies the sinner. In his own faithfulness he incorporated all the children of Promise who would eventually recognise in Christ's death the perfect restoration of divine justice.

While the figures and types of the Old Testament do not explain away the mystery of redemption nor explain *how* the crucifixion restored the equilibrium between heaven and earth, they do provide categories for contemplating it. They appeal to the poetic imagination, draw upon the artistic tradition, rely on the power of signs – as Jesus himself did – to communicate the substance of truth which is attained more through prayer than philosophy, through contrition more than legal perfection, through gratitude rather than self-righteousness.

In contemplating the mystery of salvation through the symbolism of the poetic imagination Christians use scripture not simply to explore the pathos of Christ's passion but to sound the depths of divine mercy to an unworthy race. As before – an impossible task methodologically without the help of a lesser example closer to ground-level experience. Moreover, we do not always need a text whose meaning is, properly speaking, typical or figurative in the exegetical sense. Often an accommodated reading of a passage whose relevance to the cross is not explicit will serve the contemplative's purpose. Such a case is the history of David and Absalom.

We are not dealing here with allegory as in the parables of Jesus for example, where each character and element relates directly to an underlying moral truth. There are no mystical types that match historical figures in the New Testament; nor any prophetic foretelling of Calvary; nor is this the first act of a dramatic plot that finds its denouement in the gospels. The chronicles of the Kings of Israel – however edited to suit theological purpose – are fundamentally history and as such have a process of their own. Factually they merit interest by recording how Israel as a nation came to be and to grow through various forms of political and religious organisation. Though God's hand was in the making and shaping, the telling of the story submits to all the constraints of written history; it contains its significance within itself even allowing for hindsight and the interpretation of the historian.

Nevertheless because this is Bible history it bears the imprint of revelation. Stamped with the same truth-value as the other sacred books, it constitutes part of God's dealings with his Chosen People and furthers the great themes of Election, Promise and Fulfilment that concern this tradition.

Given this, we have in David's lament for Absalom the full Biblical measure of true paternal love, a clear reflection of an ideal whose source is God himself from whom all fatherhood takes its name (Eph. 3:15). YHWH's compassion was reserved not just for his beloved sons but for his delinquent ones as well. They drew his deepest pity to themselves for they needed it most. Hence David's vulnerability at the loss of his wayward Absalom could not have been more acute if he had lost his loyal Solomon. In this is the transcendent love of perfect fatherhood conceptualised.

At its source such love is entirely faithful. It makes no distinction between its progeny on the grounds of merit. Incredibly, the children of the Fall are as highly valued as the naturally-Begotten since what is perfect knows no division in its affection. As Jesus once remarked in a different context, 'If you, then, who are evil, know how to give good gifts to your children, how much more will the heavenly Father give the Holy Spirit to those who ask him' (Luke 11:13). The Spirit is the Personal affection of God for all alike. It is his Breath, prefigured, that we hear in the sobbing of David over the gate at Jerusalem.

For sure Absalom deserved his fate. From whichever perspective we view his actions – that of natural justice, or family ties, Sovereign loyalty, patriotic duty, social responsibility or moral rectitude – he was guilty. Yet the King never intended him to pay the ultimate price for his rebellion. Even as David marshalls his troops to quell the uprising, his plea for his son's safety takes the form of a royal imperative. 'The king ordered Joab and Abishai and Ittai, "Deal gently for my sake with the young man Absalom". And all the people heard when the king gave orders to all the commanders about Absalom' (2 Sam. 18:5). The instruction was recalled and repeated in the crisis of battle by an unnamed soldier who was ordered to slay the traitor. 'The man said to Joab, "Even if I felt in my hand the weight of a thousand pieces of silver, I would not put forth my hand against the king's son; for in our hearing the king commanded you and Abishai and Ittai, For my sake protect the young man Absalom".' (2 Sam. 18:12)

In Joab's retort – 'I will not waste time like this with you' (2 Sam. 18:14) – the voice of social justice and political expediency prevails, so he executes the renegade himself. Defending his action later he spares no thought for his master's gentler feelings but openly scorns the royal tears: ' "You have today covered with shame the faces of all your servants, who have this day saved your life . . . because you love those who hate you" ' (2 Sam. 18:5–6). Expediency at that moment meant nothing to David. Though King, he was first a father. Whatever wrong his son had done, however just the punishment, his grief was uncontrollable. It overflowed in a paroxysm of pain in a scene that is unparalleled in the Bible.

> The king said to the Cushite, 'Is it well with the young man Absalom?' And the Cushite answered, 'May the enemies of my lord the king, and all who rise up against you for evil, be like that young man.' And the king was deeply moved, and went up to the chamber over the gate,

29

and wept; and as he went, he said, 'O my son Absalom, my son, my son Absalom! Would that I had died instead of you, O Absalom, my son, my son!' It was told Joab, 'Behold the king is weeping and mourning for Absalom.' So the victory that day was turned into mourning for all the people; for the people heard that day, 'The king is grieving for his son.' And the people stole into the city that day as people steal in who are ashamed when they flee in battle. The king covered his face, and the king cried with a loud voice, 'O my son Absalom, O Absalom, my son, my son!' (2 Sam. 18:32–19:4)

If natural fatherly affection overrides the legitimate demands of justice so that David's dismay was greater at the punishment than the crime, how much more is this true of supernatural Fatherhood. God's justice is a paternal justice. It is not satisfied by retribution but by forgiveness. David's forgiveness was no detached, juridical concession. It was a full-blooded, passionate obsession. His actual words were: 'Would that I had died instead of you!' Could God's empathy be any less? If the sublime words of David, though futile, are Revelation's echo of the Voice that fathered all creation, might not the Omnipotent Word carry out sublimely for his renegade creation what David could not? *'Would that I had died instead of you!'*

No scribe of the old dispensation would have dared pursue the idea. He would not even have had the imagination to do so. He would however have recognised in the faithless Absalom an image of sinful Israel corporately considered as God's ungrateful son; would have heard in David's lament, YHWH's call to repentance; would have seen in the young man's fate, Israel's rightful due. The prophets after all never tired of warning the rebellious race that unless they returned

they would perish. 'If you rebel,' cautioned Isaiah, 'you shall
be devoured by the sword' (1:20). Ezekiel likewise: 'When a
righteous man turns away from his righteousness and commits
iniquity . . . shall he live?. . . For the treachery of which he is
guilty and the sin he has committed, he shall die' (18:24).
Absalom's end proved the prophetic word true. Indeed the
particular violence of his annihilation emphasised the urgency
of the warning.

> Absalom was riding upon his mule, and the mule went
> under the thick branches of a great oak, and his head
> caught fast in the oak, and he was left hanging between
> heaven and earth, while the mule that was under him went
> on. . . . And (Joab) took three darts in his hand, and thrust
> them into the heart of Absalom, while he was still alive
> in the oak. And ten young men, Joab's armour-bearers,
> surrounded him, and killed him. . . .
>
> And they took Absalom, and threw him into a great pit
> in the forest, and raised over him a very great heap of
> stones. (2 Sam. 18:9; 14–17)

What no Old Testament scribe could possibly have dreamed
was that such a scene would one day in substance describe the
death and burial of Jesus.

In Christ's passion the full reality of universal fatherhood
was exposed as it is, the absolute antitype of all fatherly
compulsion to rescue one's child even at the expense of one's
self. God's gentle dealing with his wayward Absalom, the
Church, achieved what David could only yearn for but never
achieve: the transfer of the other's death-guilt on to his own
shoulders as a burden of love. This is the great Cosmic Truth
whose holy obsession with salvation is mirrored in every
father's pain at the loss of a child unreconciled.

If St Paul was not thinking of David's words over Absalom when he wrote his Letter to the Romans, he was certainly thinking of the absolute selflessness of the divine mercy whose spirit David shared on the human level. Probing the depths of God's love for the unrighteous, he points out that

> we were still helpless when at his appointed moment Christ died for sinful men. It is not easy to die even for a good man . . . but what proves that God loves us is that Christ died for us while we were still sinners. (5:6–8. JB)

That the mercy of God is deeper yet is indicated by the ironic twist to the full reality which the David story does not prepare us for. It was Christ who died, not the Father. God's righteous Son for his unrighteous sons. Not even David in his stricken extremity would have allowed such an exchange. To forfeit one's own life is conceivable, but to sacrifice an innocent second person would simply have re-located the grief, not eliminated it.

The illogicality of God's action is not relieved by further explanation other than to say with St John that 'God *is* love' and that 'God's love for us was revealed when God sent into the world his Son to be the sacrifice that takes our sins away . . . so that we could have life through him' (1 John 4:8; 16; 10; 9. JB). In other words, it is in the nature of the mystery of God to do what dumbfounds the world, always remembering that 'God's foolishness is wiser than human wisdom' and that therefore 'the language of the cross may be illogical to those who are not on the way to salvation, but those of us who are on the way see it as God's power to save' (1 Cor. 1:25; 18. JB).

It is precisely because we are dealing here with incomprehensible mystery, ultimate reality, absolute antitype that will never be within the range of present understanding, that we require articulate models of lesser truth to ground a discussion on the nature of the cross. Not that these models enclose Christ's relationship with God – for nothing can contain the Beyond; but they do *dis*-close the Eternal, open up the mystical union of God within himself and reveal how we are drawn into that saving unity through the holiness that human nature attains when it becomes conscious of ineffable love.

However while the Old Testament may prepare us for this dis-closure, it does not unite us with it. It requires the New Testament to do that. This is because there is a qualitative difference between the reality we are talking about and all its foreshadowings, types, prefigurements, just as there is a fundamental difference between our communion with the mystery through the gospel and our familiarity with its historical and literary images. In this sense there is real discontinuity between the old and new dispensations as well as a continuum. What Christ reveals is something really new, a transformation of the types, of our perception of his Father's love, and ultimately of ourselves. His cross is the epicentre of the new order that surfaces out of the old, as different in its fulfilment as a new creation is different from the tremors that announce it: Calvary challenges every notion of God that tries to petrify his Fatherhood in the magma of purely natural experience.

The crucifixion demonstrates that the love which sent Christ to his fate is not a love that re-acts, but that acts. It does not retaliate, it reaches out to sinners. Recognising weakness, it responds. Therefore it is subject to nothing but itself. God's Fatherliness is free for example from moral dilemma, which human fatherhood is not. It is not constrained by emotion, which causes men to hesitate. It is untouched by confusion or uncertainty which in us enfeebles and hinders the will to act. It is aware of causes and consequences – of which we frequently are not – perceiving the total good which is its sole aim and of whose accomplishment it is perfectly sure. Thus while Abraham and David lead us towards a concept of ideal paternity, they remain models of human perfection, not divine. If they anticipate at all what is to come, it is only by falling short. By giving a measure of the most that men can achieve, they indicate the immeasurability of what God has done. Like Fray Juan de la Cruz, they change our perspective on fatherhood itself by falling far below the reality above, which *willingly* ordained that the Son should suffer.

When St John of the Cross's small drawing of Calvary was shown to the painter Jose Maria Sert, it is said he at once turned it sideways. Perspective was changed yet again. This time the crucified Christ fell forward, limbs stretched to breaking-point, head bowed, in the attitude in which a crucifix might be placed by a monk on the lips of a dying man. The power and originality of the drawing were suddenly redoubled. The point of the passion became clear. Through his Son the Father touches his sons, takes to himself their sufferings, absorbs their dying, purifies their guilt. Through Christ's falling-forward, his stretching, his bowing down, the perfect freedom of God's act is affirmed. This is no reluctant sacrifice like Abraham's, no tragic misfortune like David's. Christ's crucified humanity is the sacrament of God's terrifying compassion for his creation. The visible sign of the Father's invisible straining towards what would otherwise be lost. Jesus' perfect obedience as man shows us, enfleshed, perfect co-operation between Father and Son in the undivided unity of the divine will.

That God's paternity is different from any other becomes

apparent by a distinctive change in the thematic motif that is stamped on the Bible's treatment of fathers and sons. That motif in Genesis, as we have seen, was heavy with pathos. For Abraham, the child Isaac was 'Your son, your only son'. In Second Samuel the acclamation is overlaid with grief as well, hence David's tragic cry for Absalom, 'My son, my son!'. But when we pass from Hebrew to Christian scripture the tone of the motif is different. What the Father's voice from heaven proclaims over Jesus on earth in the synoptic gospels is a serene and simple acknowledgement: 'You are my beloved Son; with you I am well pleased' (Mark 1:11).

The statement is warm and tender, full of fatherly pride, calm and supportive. It is also a quotation from the first of four Songs of God's Suffering Servant, texts from the prophet Isaiah that promised one who would take away his people's sin by enduring great pain. All four texts register YHWH's approval of that Servant's task; his endurance was God's will. Similarly in the gospels. The voice of the Father confirms the purpose of Jesus' mission. He is the one who, by his obedience unto death, will wash away the world's iniquity. The spoken motif verifies that in the Son the Father's plan is running its course. Even more, that the Son *is* the plan once hidden, now revealed, and that therefore his sorrowful destiny not only has his Father's consent, but serves his express command.

The context in which the motif is sounded endorses the point. It occurs at crucial moments in the story of Jesus when the theme of his passion is introduced or repeated. At the baptism in the river Jordan for example, and at the transfiguration. In the first instance, Jesus has just emerged from the water at the hands of John the Baptiser. As he rises up the heavens open and the voice of the Father resounds over the surface of the deep. It is the moment of Jesus' anointing as the Christ, the Messiah ordained to cleanse the creation by stemming the ancient flood-water of sin. The baptism is a symbolic action. It enacts the means by which he will achieve his aim: by descent into the troubled waters of the human condition, into the experience of man's death and interment; and immediate ascent again to new life, taking with him redeemed human nature in the mystery of resurrection and ascension. To all of this the Father gives his 'Yes', as St Paul explained to the Corinthians. 'The Son of God, Jesus Christ, . . . was not Yes and No; but in him it is always Yes. For all the promises of God find their Yes in him' (2 Cor. 1:19–20).

What this implies is that Jesus' 'Yes' to God, is God's 'Yes' to us. This is why the plan formed by the Father indispensably required the Son's co-operation at Calvary. The death that Jesus accepted was our death. Had he not died we should have perished. God could no more tolerate that eventuality than David the loss of Absalom, or Abraham the death of Isaac. But unlike the Patriarchs, the heavenly Father – to spare the unworthy son – willingly yielded his faithful One that all might be saved. From this we can only conclude that God's love for his people is synonymous with his love for Christ. Jesus affirmed as much on the night before he died when he explained the reason for his coming: 'that the love with which you have loved me, O righteous Father, may be in them' (John 17:26).

In the second instance – at the transfiguration – the point was made again. The appearance of Moses and Elijah with Jesus on the mountain shows that he is the culmination of God's revelation through law and prophecy. Together they speak of 'his passing which he was to accomplish' (Luke 9:31. JB). It is to be the new passover, like the one Moses accomplished only greater. Jesus is the Deliverer promised through the prophets, though mightier than Elijah. Moses could merely liberate from Pharaoh; Jesus would break the bonds of Satan. Elijah ascended to heaven alone in his fiery chariot; Jesus would return to the Father taking all humanity with him.

As before at the Jordan, the voice from the cloud affirms the significance of the tableau: 'This is my Son, my Chosen; listen to him!' (9:35). The cloud and the mountain are Old Testament shorthand for the presence of God and his closeness to man. Here God has come down to men in Christ; the plan of salvation is ratified and witnessed. Included in the scene are the three key disciples: Peter, James and John. The New Testament bears witness as well. So must the Church, of which these are the founding members. Their message will go out to the ends of the earth. Hence the whole of sacred scripture and the whole of sacred tradition will combine to attest the veracity of what was seen and heard: that Christ is the centre not just of the tableau, not only of the theophany, but of all that God ever revealed from the beginning of time to save his creature-child.

If the event of the baptism underscored the pain of the cross in God's will, the transfiguration emphasised the glory of it. The external details persuade us this is so. The appearance of Jesus' face was altered (Luke 9:29). In Matthew's account, it 'shone like the sun' (Matt. 17:2). His clothes became 'white as light' (Matthew), 'dazzling white' (Luke), so that the mere mortals present were overcome with awe. The context of the event persuades us too. It occurred after 'eight days' (Luke 9:28), that is, seven days after the first day of the week with its associations of the resurrection. It also occurred straight after Jesus' first confiding to his disciples the news of his death in

Jerusalem and its aftermath. To console them, he permitted a glimpse of its radiant purposefulness. More bedazzling than anything seen by Ezekiel on the banks of the Chebar, as superb as that which would be seen by the Presbyter of the Apocalypse, the apostles beheld in the glory of the cross what no prophet or law could show them: the pure benevolence of the Father shining on the features of the Son.

When we come to John's Gospel, the triptych is opened back complete. Here it is all glory as Jesus prepares for his arrest. We are towards the end of the story – just as the baptism began it, and the transfiguration centred it for us. The splendour is not limited to a short spell in a river, on a mountain. Nor is it confined to any time on earth. This is the eternal glory of the Son with the Father which he had before the foundation of the world. It is to be manifested in the heroic death which will unleash the glory of an heroic life. Written long after the synoptics and Golgotha itself, the motif this time has a power and a form all its own.

> 'For this purpose I have come to this hour. Father, glorify thy name.' Then a voice came from heaven, 'I have glorified it, and I will glorify it again.' The crowd standing by heard it and said that it had thundered. . . . Jesus answered, 'This voice has come for your sake, not for mine. Now is the judgment of this world, now shall the ruler of this world be cast out; and I, when I am lifted up from the earth, will draw all men to myself.' (John 12:27–32)

Thenceforth, the Father's voice falls silent. It fails to come again. Now there is only his Word, hanging limp from the wood of the cross-beam. In Jesus crucified is all God's speech. He proclaims by his open arms, the gaping wounds, his lanced side, his abject state, the entirety of our Father's discourse to us. In the dread silence of this fulness of speech, it is left to the centurion of the earliest gospel tradition – that which was still most vivid when written down – to reverberate what cannot be unsaid. 'Truly this was the Son of God' (Mark 15:39; Matt. 27:54). On the lips of a Gentile the Fatherhood of Jesus' God would be proclaimed along every road of the Roman Empire; that God so loved the world, he sacrificed his only Son; that the Son so loved his Father, he emptied himself and became obedient unto death. This proclamation, this *kerygma*, would break through every barrier; it would transcend time; it would pierce eternity, destroy the power of death, rout the forces of evil, create a new heaven and a new earth, and establish God's reign forever.

In the final phase of that plan, the centurion's motif becomes an act of faith for the nations. His words however do not refer to Jesus alone for he is the head of a body that is incomplete without its members. St Paul stressed the idea from the earliest days and demonstrated its implications. 'Just as the body is one and has many members, and all the members of the body, though many, are one body, so it is with Christ. . . . Now you are the body of Christ and individually members of it' (1 Cor. 12:12; 27). After Christ, no one can speak of God's Beloved Son again apart from the Christian Community. The christological motif is now a self-identifying acclamation of faith for the Church. What Christ is, it is. And since Christ is identified by Calvary – fullest exposition of Beloved Sonship – then Calvary will always be the sign by which the Church is recognised too. It cannot be otherwise because the cross is proof of the Father's perfect love for his only Son, members and head united, unique and inseparable.

That the Beloved Son identifies himself most of all with those who suffer was made clear to Paul on the road to

Damascus. The voice that came from heaven this time was that of Jesus himself. 'Saul, Saul, why do you persecute me?' (Acts 9:4). When Paul asked, 'Who are you?' the answer should have been: 'The Christians of Damascus and Jerusalem' – for these were the object of his attack. The response however – 'I am Jesus, whom you are persecuting' (Acts 9:5) – echoed and endorsed the other *ipsissima verba* that Matthew recorded, 'Truly I say to you, as you did it to one of the least of these my brothers, you did it to me' (25:40).

Wherever there is pain, there is the Beloved Sonship. As once God looked into the creature he had formed and loved the beauty reflected there of his own image before the Fall, so now, gazing into the eyes of all who suffer he beholds his perfect image restored – more splendid than ever; for there he finds the Crucified, on whom the divine pity rests.

This is what St Paul meant when, speaking of Christian initiation, he asked: 'Do you not know that all of us who have been baptized into Christ Jesus were baptized into his death? We were buried therefore with him by baptism into death. . . . We have been united with him in a death like his' (Rom. 6:3–5). The cross must be extended through the ages just as the divine Sonship must by sharing in Christ's Spirit in the Church. Golgotha is not a past event. It will never be complete until the body of Christ is complete, fully formed in every limb. The passion must run to the body's extremities before the full complement of the redeemed can be numbered. Like any man, Christ knows his body best through the pain of its parts.

A consciousness of this gave Paul's sufferings a new meaning for him. 'Now I rejoice in my sufferings for your sake, and in my flesh I complete what is lacking in Christ's afflictions for the sake of his body, that is, the church' (Col.

1:24). How could Christ's afflictions be lacking in any way, unless the mystical communion between his physical body and his ecclesial body is real? Since that communion is not a metaphor, not two realities but one; since the Son of God can have only one body, and that body *is* the Church, then in a real sense his afflictions are lacking until they be reproduced in every Christian. Where the Church has not yet suffered it has not been conformed to the reality of its sonship, it is not yet known to Christ.

Putting the matter positively, the cross teaches that there is beauty in pain. Not because pain is beautiful, but because it has been transfigured by the love of God, transfused with Christ's blood. It has power to unite God and man, to humanise, to deify. Christ is present in pain so that all who suffer might be present in him. Since the Church is a mystical union with God through affliction, then all who bear affliction for love's sake are baptised into Christ, are members of his Church, and are therefore saved.

What this means is that not only is the Father invisibly present at Calvary; so also are we. As in the union between Father and Son Calvary unites time and eternity, so in the union between Christ and us it unites age with age. In this way the cross transcends any single epoch of history, entering into all of it through Christ's suffering members. But more: since by sharing Christ's crucifixion all generations become with him God's only Son, we experience directed towards us the entire, undivided love of God for the Only-begotten. It was after all for this that the Father permitted the head to suffer for the whole body – having made him head for that very purpose; by the same token it is for the sake of the head that the Father allows the members, who must suffer on account of sin, to become under Christ one Christ that the

41

Son might be all in all. Thus all have been given to him because he suffered for all. They belong to him because in him they have suffered too.

This is why Jesus is called the Mediator. He hangs between heaven and earth uniting both in himself. He is stretched out from age to age, drawing all time into his eternity. In him crucified we find the Father; in him reigning from the cross we find ourselves. In all respects he is the centre of salvation.

Whoever therefore looks at the cross and recognises in it his own pain, merits the eternal Father's tenderness for the dying Christ. And whoever, feeling that tenderness towards him, recognises Christ in himself, knows that he does not suffer alone. He will see all he endures swept up in a passion greater than his own, carrying him straight into the passionate heart of the Trinity where the love of God, accepting all that is darkest, is transforming the universe into glory and unveiling that glory as the kingdom.

It is with this in mind that we turn to the three gospel traditions of Christ's dark glory, starting with that recorded by Mark-Matthew.

CHAPTER TWO

'My God! My God!'

The Mark-Matthew Passion Tradition

THE MOST REMARKABLE feature of the earliest account of the passion – that which distinguishes the tradition of Mark and Matthew from the others – is Jesus' utter silence during his suffering. St Luke's Christ waxes eloquent from the cross: to the good thief as to the women of Jerusalem before that, and to his heavenly Father at his resigned end. In St John his words are memorable for their serene and perfect poise. But in Matthew, whose source is Mark's account (written well within living memory of the event), there are no words of wisdom, no farewell speeches from the gallows, no purposeful sayings to relieve the catastrophe, no verbal consolations of forgiveness. Nothing but a complete silence from the trial before Pilate until mid-afternoon when the darkness that covered the earth was pierced by an appalling scream of pain, an inarticulate cry that sounded like abject despair.

This silence is not accidental. Both Mark and Matthew draw attention to it more than once. Not only by the sparsity of direct speech attributed to Jesus after Gethsemane, but also by Pilate's quiet amazement at the fact.

> When [Jesus] was accused by the chief priests and elders, he made no answer. Then Pilate said to him, 'Do you not

hear how many things they testify against you?' But he gave him no answer, not even to a single charge; so that the governor wondered greatly. (Matt. 27:12–14)

Earlier, before Caiaphas, Jesus maintained the same defence-lessness as the false witnesses gave their testimony. He spoke only when the high priest put him under oath to answer, and then qualified his statement about his divine Sonship by stressing his identity as Son of Man, his preferred title denoting humility and personal impoverishment. Under torture at the praetorium, when a whole battalion of Pilate's henchmen attacked him at once, he never opened his mouth. When he tasted the sponge soaked in gall, though dehydrated he said not a word. When they taunted and jibed his crucified form, and dared him come down off the cross, he did not respond. His only sound – the high-pitched, slurred keening – was wrought involuntarily by the death-throes of a soul thoroughly riddled and sifted by suffering.

That we, like Pilate, should find such silence stunning is understandable. What man could stand by speechless when accused? Especially if he were innocent? Even if one were guilty one would attempt some sort of self-defence. To do so is a natural instinct as well as a legal right. In the case of false accusation the instinct is doubly strong. As a matter of justice one would feel impelled to speak out. It would happen spon-taneously. Mind and heart together would automatically find a voice. Psalm 38 (39) describes in very human terms the inner struggle that would take place were one to attempt to say nothing.

I said: 'I will be watchful of my ways
for fear I should sin with my tongue.
I will put a curb on my lips

when the wicked man stands before me'.
(And yet:)
My heart was burning within me.
At the thought of it, the fire blazed up
and my tongue burst into speech. . . .

The speech of this unnamed victim however was addressed to
God, not to his persecutor, and so

(Though) his prosperity stirred my grief,
I was dumb, silent and still.
I was silent, not opening my lips,
because this (O God) was all your doing.

By his unusual patience under stress and by his evident innocence, this man is a type of Christ, a prefigurement of Jesus.
His case is similar too in that he recognised the hand of God
in what he was being asked to bear. Nevertheless Jesus' silence
is not adequately explained by Psalm 38. In his lifetime he was
often regaled with abuse by the scribes and Pharisees; he never
allowed them the last word. In every instance he refuted their
insidious remarks, rebuffed their lies, exposed their malice.
His consistent acceptance of all verbal challenge therefore
makes his speechless passion particularly poignant. Even if his
suffering 'was all God's doing', why should he not register
some remark as he was always wont to do, at least to instruct
his disciples who would later reflect on his heroism?

A number of possibilities immediately suggest themselves,
since silence can denote many things. Perhaps Jesus was in a
state of shock. He had after all endured a deep mental crisis in
the garden; Mark recalls that he was 'greatly distressed and
troubled. And he said to them, "My soul is very sorrowful,
even to death"' (14:33–34). He had passed a night without

sleep. His friends had betrayed, denied and deserted him. His arrest was a violent affair. At least two trials were arranged in quick succession whose verdict of guilt was a foregone conclusion before they took place. Though healthy, Jesus' nature was human. What man could withstand such treatment?

This explanation however is not feasible. Throughout the entire episode Jesus was articulate in prayer and coherent to the disciples and to Caiaphas. His mind was not deranged. Perhaps then his silence concealed scorn? When defeated by an unjust judgement, one line of defence is to ignore the judge. One tries to maintain one's dignity by treating the accuser with indifference, contempt, as if he did not exist. This too is unacceptable. Jesus never treated anyone with malice. He was incapable of such an emotion.

Is it possible that Jesus had despaired of his fate, grown tired of running from inevitable arrest, had simply resigned himself wearily to the destiny that was bound to be his sooner or later? He knew they had planned to capture him many times, had plotted his death long before but refrained from doing so because of the crowds. Does there come a time, even for the Son of God, when deliverance from destiny no longer seems viable? Hardly. Matthew's embellishment of Mark's account of the arrest suggests that he freely entered into his fate because the moment was mature for his final task. 'Then Jesus said to [Peter], "Put your sword back into its place. . . . Do you think that I cannot appeal to my Father, and he will at once send me more than twelve legions of angels? But how then should the scriptures be fulfilled, that it must be so?"' (Matt. 26:52–54). What was happening was not beyond his control. It was very much in line with what had been planned and foretold.

The true explanation is given by St Paul who revealed it to

the Corinthians in writing even before the Gospels of Mark or Matthew were composed on papyrus. Jesus was silent before his accusers quite simply *because he was guilty.* Not of the crimes whipped up by their malign imagination but – much worse – of all the crimes of sinful humanity from the beginning of time.

> For our sake [God] made him to be sin who knew no sin, so that in him we might become the righteousness of God.
>
> (2 Cor. 5:21)

The theology was not Paul's alone. It was the common faith of the Christian communities that had broken through the borders of Judaism and were spreading through Asia Minor and into Europe, but which constituted one Church by their unity of belief in what God had accomplished in Christ. This faith was consistent with its Jewish roots. Psalm 38 (39) again for example had already paved the way for such an understanding.

> [O Lord] set me free from all my sins,
> do not make me the taunt of the fool. . . .
> Take away your scourge from me.
> I am crushed by the blows of your hand.
> You punish man's sins and correct him. . . .
>
> Look away that I may breathe again
> before I depart to be no more.

The sins that Christ was guilty of were not his own. But he made them his own by becoming man, by becoming head of his body the Church. This was not his own will, but the Father's. Hence the agony in Gethsemane. As God's Beloved Son he was faultless. Yet as man he was sent to embrace a humanity contaminated by sin. Proceeding from perfect Love, how could he reject the creature made through him and for him? Yet being perfect Love, how could he embrace what had become sinful? For God in himself, in his divine nature, this was no problem. But for God in a human nature, this was crucifixion. The human will of Jesus the Nazarene recoiled from the conflict with the greatest fear and trembling. His divine will however subjected all his earthly reservations to God's plan and so he assumed the entire guilt of all who ever failed to love as God loves. Jesus' silence on Good Friday was not merely the act of a patient man. It was the act of a divine man facing up to the consequences of his incarnation.

To appreciate the meaning of Christ's dumbness at the end one needs to reflect on the speech of his life, both his words and his actions. These explain the purpose of his passion, his quiet acceptance of it, more eloquently than any comment could. One of the early Fathers, Ignatius of Antioch, put the point very succinctly in the second century:

> It is better to keep quiet and be, than to make fluent professions and not be. No doubt it is a fine thing to instruct others, but only if the speaker practises what he preaches. One such teacher there is: 'he who spake the word, and it was done'; and what he achieved even by his silences was well worthy of the Father. A man who has truly mastered the utterances of Jesus will also be able to apprehend his silence, and thus reach full spiritual maturity, so that his own words have the force of actions and his silences the significance of speech.
>
> (*To the Ephesians*, §15)

Jesus' whole existence on earth testified to his solidarity with sinners and his commitment to God. As he lived so he died. If action speaks louder than words, passion speaks loudest of all. Action, passion and speech joined forces with a singleness of purpose in the Word made flesh to demonstrate the Father's care for the world he had made. Such was Paul's perception of the situation in the passage to the Corinthinans where he asserted that Christ was made to be sin. 'That is,' he explained, 'God was in Christ reconciling the world to himself, not counting their trespasses against them' (2 Cor. 5:19). Fatherly love cannot bear estrangement.

The silence of Jesus before pain is matched in the Mark-Matthew accounts only by the silence of the Father before his dying Son. God's silence is even more remarkable than that of Christ. At least Jesus did speak – however briefly – to his beloved Father in his desperation. ' "Eloi, Eloi, lama sabachthani?" which means "My God, my God, why have you forsaken me?" ' (Mark 15:34). He used his native tongue. He was quoting God's word in the Psalms. He was at the end of his strength. But God made no reply at all. No shaft of light shone from above. No comforting angel brought him relief. His Father remained silent till it was over. Could Abraham have said nothing? Could David as Absalom hung in the oak tree?

For mystics like John of the Cross Jesus' desolation epitomises the dark night of the soul shared by many Christians since Calvary, the mystery of the innocent sufferer for whom the greatest trial is God's apparent absence. Most Christians however are not mystics. When God seems not to respond to prayer, when he seems not to care about pain, when he fails to intervene to save the good man or the child, faith itself falls silent in its inability to comprehend. Nor does the gospel attempt to explain the mystery away. Jesus alone is faith's reason for believing. He is the answer that quietens the voice of despair that would indeed prevail had Calvary not happened. For in Christ forsaken we find ourselves accepted; in Christ unanswered we hear ourselves listened to; in Christ unconsoled we feel ourselves comforted since God is in Christ facing the dark night with us and for us. If God should seem unresponsive to prayer therefore it is not because he is unconcerned, still less that he has nothing to say to us. Rather he has said it all, and said it to the full at Golgotha.

So what *is* God saying through the crucifixion of Jesus? Primarily that sin is a fearful catastrophe. The cross shows its terrible effects in the bleeding body of Christ. Here is what evil does to man even if he does not see it. Here is what evil does to God who sees it all too clearly. Christ's extreme suffering exposes injustice for what it really is: the cause of horrific rupture in the human condition that leads to great unhappiness, violence and death. Calvary convinces us of the cost of repairing injustice, even that which might be called venial. It forces us to acknowledge that no imperfection can pass unatoned for, not even that which men excuse in themselves on the grounds of weakness, and that atonement demands a shocking retribution.

Mark and Matthew portray the passion as a total devastation of Christ's manhood, at once physical, mental and spiritual. The facts speak for themselves: this is how human indifference defaces God's glory. The bare truth of it, once seen, renders the repentant – like Christ and his Father – speechless in their turn. The silence this time however is one of shocked awareness, akin to what Isaiah attributed to those who gazed on the Suffering Servant:

So shall he startle many nations;
kings shall shut their mouths because of him;
for that which has not been told them

they shall see;
and that which they have not heard
they shall understand. (52:15)

Matthew in particular had the text of this Suffering Servant
Song in mind as he handled the detail of Jesus' agony. Because
he wrote his Gospel mainly for those of a Jewish background
he expected his audience to have the Old Testament scriptures
open beside them. They would have had access therefore to
Isaiah's vivid description of the brutal physical condition of the
unnamed victim.

Behold, my servant shall prosper,
he shall be exalted and lifted up,
and shall be very high.
As many were astonished at him –
his appearance was so marred,
beyond human semblance,
and his form beyond that of the sons of men –
so shall he startle many nations. . . .

He had no form or comeliness that we should look at
    him,
and no beauty that we should desire him.
He was despised and rejected by men;
a man of sorrows, and acquainted with grief;
and as one from whom men hide their faces
he was despised, and we esteemed him not.

(52:13–14; 53:2–3)

The tragic irony of the language in the opening verse here
adds to the intensity of the suffering described. 'Exalted',
'lifted up', 'very high', are terms of honour, majesty and glory.

51

Yet the context shows that the opposite is meant. In Matthew's crucifixion the uplifting is that of the *patibulum* or cross-beam, rudely hoisted and jerked on to the vertical stake that was permanently positioned on Calvary. The 'very high' degree of pain that ensued sickeningly contradicts the notion of laurels of distinction. Christ's 'exalted' status, his helpless dangling from a gallows, crudely dismisses the thought of any dais of victory.

Two voices intone the text of Isaiah's song. The first is that of YHWH; the other, that of the people. The mysterious Servant hangs mutely between them, centred, pinned, transfixed in anguish between his God above and his people below. Like that Servant pre-cast in the image of the Son, the Jesus of Matthew and Mark is so 'marred', so lacking now in 'comeliness' or 'beauty' that his appearance no longer bears 'human resemblance', 'his form' no longer resembles 'that of the sons of men'. When his torturers have finished with him he is not recognisable even to his relatives. Exposed before the gaze of God and men, he is a stranger to both.

How vulnerable is the human body! The slightest knock causes magnificent swelling. Jesus was beaten round the head and face. His eyes would have been puffed out and bruised. The nose broken and distorted. The lips of his mouth parched and chaffed. Rivulets of blood amassing in caked pools around his bearded throat. The skin of his face pale and sallow as parchment. His neck and shoulders limp. One thinks of a road accident victim. So badly disfigured that the coffin is kept closed out of respect for the mourners' sensitivity. Not so with Christ. His brutalised frame was pilloried and lampooned while he was yet alive to add to his degradation. Displayed in its very worst appearance that he might be spared nothing while the breath remained in his body.

That breath did not remain long. Jesus' death was swift in comparison with that of other victims. It occurred in a matter of hours rather than days as was usual. Pilate was surprised when they came to request Christ's corpse. 'Joseph of Arimathea . . . took courage and went to Pilate, and asked for the body of Jesus. And Pilate wondered if he were already dead; and summoning the centurion, he asked whether he was already dead. And when he learned from the centurion that he was dead, he granted the body to Joseph' (Mark 15:43–45). The robbers executed with Jesus were still alive as the sun was setting. They had to be killed to clear the site before the sabbath.

What this clearly reveals is the hidden extent of Christ's injuries. His unusual patience before his torturers concealed the full effects of the flailing. Exhausted, the weight of his scourged body would have made it impossible to breathe on the cross. He would have had to heave himself up to get a breath. The effort would have strained the wounds on his feet. It would have drained the little energy that was left. His frame would have slumped again in moments. The heavy drag would have torn at the nails in his wrists. It would have blocked respiration again. And so the process would have continued over and over: the upward exertion for air, the downward collapse for want of strength, until all physical resources were spent. In the end Christ died of asphyxiation as the last breath gurgled out of him with the desperate, suffocating cry.

The evangelists are silent about the interior working of Jesus' mind or emotions. Their reporting is gravely objective. But both relied heavily on two of the psalms as they reconstructed the passion, and those psalms – numbers 21 and 68 (known by heart to the earliest Jewish-Christians) – offer intense psychological insight into the agonised mind of one

53

who has suffered more than is bearable. In the light of these texts, the Gospels' deliberate omission of any overt comment on Jesus' mental state is a sombre reminder that some facts are so dreadful they are better left unrecorded.

Many bulls have surrounded me,
fierce bulls of Bashan close me in.
Against me they open wide their jaws,
like lions, rending and roaring.

Like water I am poured out,
disjointed are all my bones.
My heart has become like wax,
it is melted within my breast.

Parched as burnt clay is my throat,
my tongue cleaves to my jaws.
Many dogs have surrounded me,
a band of the wicked beset me.
They tear holes in my hands and my feet
and lay me in the dust of death.

I can count every one of my bones.
These people stare at me and gloat;
they divide my clothing among them.
They cast lots for my robe. . . .

O Lord, rescue . . . my life from the grip of these dogs.
Save my soul from the jaws of these lions,
my poor soul from the horns of these oxen.

(Ps. 21/22)

The nightmarish symbolism of the animals expresses the sub-

54

conscious horror of the mind under physical attack. Fierce
bulls, roaring lions, many dogs, horned oxen – and then the
dogs and the lions again, repeated – constitute a full circle of
terrifying images from which there is no escape. The soul
recoils at the wholesale nature of the threat. The entire man is
about to be devoured. *Psyche* and *soma* in one, he is utterly
trapped in the gyrating assault on the body. Around him all is
snapping, snarling, teeth-baring, fang-displaying. The
monsters spring forward for the mangling, the tearing, the
ripping-open of the soul itself. For when the flesh is ravaged,
mind and spirit and soul are equally mauled and pulled apart.
One's devastation is total.

Read in the light of Mark-Matthew's accounts – as the
evangelists intended they should be – the psalms therefore
suggest that Christ's mental trauma was even greater than his
physical ordeal. Purely physical pain, once over, may in time
be forgotten; mental and emotional affliction on the other
hand leave their scarred remains forever.

> More numerous than the hairs on my head
> are those who hate me without cause.
> Those who attack me with lies are too much for my
> strength.
>
> . . . I have become a stranger to my brothers,
> an alien to my own mother's sons. . . .
>
> Do not hide your face [O Lord] from your servant;
> answer quickly for I am in distress.
> Come close to my soul and redeem me;
> ransom me pressed by my foes.

You know how they taunt and deride me;
my oppressors are all before you.
Taunts have broken my heart;
I have reached the end of my strength.
I looked in vain for compassion,
for consolers; not one could I find.

(Ps. 68/69)

To read these lines is to read the mind of Christ, isolated and desolate. Excruciating suffering is one thing, but to know that one's pain is willed by others is something else. The sense of this began for him in the Garden of Gethsemane. It produced a desperate loneliness that in a lesser man would have turned to panic. In his struggle with the Father's will he rose from the ground three times to seek human consolation in the companionship of friends, but found them sleeping. At his arrest when he needed them most, they fled. 'I looked in vain for compassion, for consolers; not one could I find.'

He received no compassion from his fellow countrymen either. Not even from the Jewish authorities who should have been spiritual father to him in his time of distress. Though the Jews were united in their hatred of the Romans they lifted not a hand to protect one of their own from the oppressor. Instead they levered the political power of the detested invader to dislodge a brother Jew whom they detested more. Rome – usually so fair in its treatment even of the criminal, so traditionally proud of its justice system – was too morally weak to counter what was happening. Had Jesus hoped for protection from the stranger, even on the grounds of humanity, he would have hoped in vain.

There is no punishment greater than personal rejection. To be cut off from others, even by chance but especially by design, to be systematically despised, cast out, excoriated, is actually more than the mind can sustain. It hits directly at the essence of what it is to be human, depriving a man of the very thing that gives him his sense of worth: social intercourse. It hits directly at what is divine in a man: the need for community, wherein he is created in the image of the Many-Personed God. This is why no man can survive a concerted attack on his need for society. No matter how strong he is, he is not built to exist alone and has no lasting resources to deal with such a cruel and dehumanising punishment. But that was Jesus' fate. He was deserted by friend and foe, condemned by Jew and Gentile, scorned by his own people and by strangers, disowned by Church and State – religious authorities and political leaders alike – and finally with no one left to turn to, was abandoned even by God. Suspended on the cross between heaven and earth, acknowledged by neither and excluded from both, the figure of Isaiah's Suffering Servant had fully become flesh.

> He was despised and rejected by men;
> a man of sorrows, and acquainted with grief. . . .
> smitten by God, and afflicted. . . .
> And they made his grave with the wicked . . .
> Although he had done no violence,
> and there was no deceit in his mouth.

(Is. 53: 3,4,9)

The spiritual desolation of Jesus was undoubtedly the worst aspect of the rejection he was made to feel. The truly terrible sense that one has been cut off from God. Communion with the Lord is the one consolation that normally helps a man tolerate the difficulties of life, the prospect of death. Without the awareness of the divine Presence, without any feeling of divine solidarity, even the mildest trial becomes a source of despair. Men depend on each other for this sense of God's nearness. We make Him present to one another through one another. As Son of Man Jesus needed human contact to get in touch with the God of his people. As a good Jew he required the spiritual ministry that every sincere Israelite would hope for in the shadow of the valley of death. What made Christ's spiritual agony so intense was not just that he was deprived of this solace, but that it was deliberately withheld out of malice.

The taunting of the bystanders was proof of this. ' "He trusts in God; let God deliver him now, if he desires him" ' (Matt. 27:43). Among the group were the chief priests, with the scribes and the elders. These ministers of religion entrusted with the covenant, were the very ones who excluded him from its terms and its promises. Their indifference to his spiritual welfare became evident when they 'delivered him to Pilate the governor' (Matt. 27:2). Pilate was a Gentile and it was forbidden by the Law for an Israelite to enter the house of a foreigner during the season of Passover. It would have rendered him ritually unclean so that he could not celebrate the Feast. Since this was the most important event in the Jewish calendar, to be excommunicated from it was to be locked out of the Chosen People, God's delivered ones. By 'delivering' Jesus to the Roman governor they callously gave him up to contamination (as they saw it), leaving him to cope with the consequences of his situation as best he could. Not one of his brother Jews dared accompany him into the praetorium, which is why Pilate came out to them when he had to address the throng after Jesus had been interrogated. They were too holy at Passover to come in to him.

Even if Jesus' relationship with God was different so that he alone could call God 'Abba', and even if his attitude to the

traditions of the elders was realistically sceptical, he was no
less a child of the covenant for all that. The fact that he desired
to eat the Passover before his passion proves it. And that his
teaching was never proposed as an alternative to the holy Law
of Moses but a fulfilment of it (Matt. 5:17), proves it too.
Therefore Jesus was not unaffected by the religious insensi-
tivity towards him of the spiritual leaders of Israel. As before,
the Psalms give voice to the great anguish that Jesus himself
never articulated.

> How many are rising up against me!
> How many are saying about me:
> 'There is no help for him in God'; (Ps. 3)

> There is no one who takes my part.
> I have no means of escape,
> not one who cares for my soul. (Ps. 141/142)

The combined effect of extreme physical, mental and spiritual
hardship is even more devastating for an innocent man than a
guilty one. Only the innocent feel the supposed absence of
God, their supposed separation from him. For Christ, who
was perfectly holy, the experience was unspeakably wretched:
he had to bear in his compassionate humanity the unworthi-
ness of humanity itself. Though guilty of nothing, by the fact
that he was man he tasted the degradation of being human
after the Fall. He belonged to a race that by nature, as St Paul
put it, was under God's anger (Eph. 2:3. JB). Just by dint of
his birth he incurred God's wrath with all the rest. In the
words of St Paul again, 'God dealt with sin by sending his own
Son in a body as physical as any sinful body, and in that body
God condemned sin' (Rom. 8:3. JB).

What gave Christ the will to face his ordeal was his sense of purpose. He drew strength from the conviction that his was an atoning death. He saw his mission as a call to suffering. By suffering he would serve. And so he identified himself as Servant. Mark records a saying from the lips of the historical Jesus that confirmed the Church's understanding of Calvary, gave positive significance to what seemed Christ's tragic end. 'Jesus called (his disciples) to him and said to them . . . "Whoever would be great among you must be slave of all. *For the Son of Man also came not to be served but to serve, and to give his life as a ransom for many."* ' (10:42–45).

Although found in all the synoptics, its *source* is Mark alone. It is therefore from the most ancient Christian tradition. Even in Mark its occurrence is rare. Clearly it was a secret Jesus confided only to his closest companions. Such discretion would have been necessary in Jesus' lifetime since the idea of a *suffering* Messiah was totally unexpected to most Jews. His cryptic revelation would have been religiously preserved by the brethren in Rome in the decades up to AD 65 or so when Mark came to be written down. It indicates that Christ had always conceived his fate to be a service of redemption for sinners. The verse is directly inspired by the text of Isaiah's Fourth Suffering Servant Song, where the Servant's death is unmistakably described as a vicarious atonement for sin.

> Surely he has borne our griefs
> and carried our sorrows. . . .
> He was wounded for our transgressions,
> he was bruised for our iniquities;
> upon him was the chastisement that made us whole,
> and with his stripes we are healed. . . .
> the Lord has laid on him the iniquity of us all.

It was the will of the Lord to bruise him;
he has put him to grief;
... he makes himself an offering for sin. ...
By his knowledge shall the righteous one, my servant,
make many to be accounted righteous;
and he shall bear their iniquities. ...
He poured out his soul to death,
and was numbered with the transgressors;
yet he bore the sin of many,
and made intercession for the transgressors.

(Is. 53:4–5; 10–12)

Read all of a piece, the Song communicates more than a doctrinal truth. It conveys the moving quality of human brokenness. Through it flows the deepest current of sadness. It is a dirge that sobs and laments for the sheer pity of the Servant's condition: his humility, his perfect condescension, his total innocence, his mature yet childlike obedience, the strength of his gentleness. The emotion of the lines cannot be sustained. The writer has to look away, and then is compelled to look back again. He cannot bear to gaze on what he sees, and yet cannot bear not to. It is a vision that ends as abruptly as it began. It is too pathetic to last, too numinous to appear for long on the earth. It is the vision of the naked love of a God who, confronted with sin, strips himself of all that is his to re-clothe with his innocence the wounded nakedness of sinners.

In the after-image that follows the bright flash of that brief vision comes the second thing God is saying through the crucifixion. Not only that sin is a catastrophe, but equally that sinners should never lose heart. Since the redemption has been paid in full, none is beyond salvation. No matter how serious the offence, its power is less than that of divine mercy. To doubt this is to deny the cross, to overlook the magnitude of Christ's sufferings, to reject the Son of God a second time. Such a rejection would be even worse than the first. Perpetuated, it would constitute the sin against the Holy Spirit that Christ warned against in the gospel, the sin of despair.

It was left to the Church in the Apostolic and post-Apostolic writings to reflect on the fruitfulness of the passion. A popular theme which facilitated this reflection was the Harrowing of Hell. Based on an idea in the First Letter of Peter, it envisages Christ's soul after death descending to the underworld to proclaim his victory first to the dead who awaited liberation: 'For Christ also died for sins once for all, the righteous for the unrighteous, that he might bring us to God, being put to death in the flesh but made alive in the spirit; in which he went and preached to the spirits in prison, who formerly did not obey . . .' (3:18–20). In one ancient homily for Holy Saturday the writer develops the scenario, having Christ address Adam as his father and emphasising the brutality of the passion – as Mark and Matthew do – to bring out its power in effecting man's re-creation.

> God has died in the flesh, and the underworld has trembled. . . . He goes to free the prisoner Adam and his fellow-prisoner Eve from their pains, he who is God, and Adam's son.
>
> And Christ . . . says to Adam, 'I am your God, who for your sake became your son. . . . Arise, O man, work of my hands, arise, you who were fashioned in my image. Rise, let us go hence; for you in me and I in you, together we are one undivided person.
>
> For you, I your God became your son; for you, I the Master took on your form, that of slave; for you, I who am

above the heavens came on earth and under the earth; for you, man, I became as a man without help, free among the dead; for you, who left a garden, I was handed over to Jews from a garden and crucified in a garden.

Look at the spittle on my face, which I received because of you, in order to restore you to that first divine inbreathing at creation. See the blows on my cheeks, which I accepted in order to refashion your distorted form to my own image.

See the scourging on my back, which I accepted in order to disperse the load of your sins which was laid upon your back. See my hands nailed to the tree for a good purpose, for you, who stretched out your hand to the tree for an evil one. (*The Divine Office*, vol. II, pp. 321–322)

Three times the homilist draws attention to Christ as Adam's son. For the sake of sinful man – which is what the Hebrew 'Adam' means – the Son of God left his filial home of glory to call his creature 'father'. Bearing the weight of his parent's fault, he became the Child obedient to the needs of all incarcerated in original sin. Exchanging the society of his heavenly Father whom he loved for the company of his earthly parentage whom he created, he gave to an undeserving race the incomparable privilege of making their own his Father's words of him: Behold, here is my Beloved Son!

It was through his suffering, the Letter to the Hebrews tells us, that he learned his obedience as Son (5:8). As Son of God and Son of Man, what he endured at Golgotha made him 'the source of eternal salvation to all who obey him' (Heb. 5:9). Thus at Calvary the Child became Father to the man a second time, generating from his powerful innocence as Adam's Son, divine Sonship once again in his father's race. As at the beginning in filial obedience to the Creator the Word had brought forth God's human child in original grace, so now in filial obedience to fallen Adam's cry, he restored graced childhood to his earthly parent's nature through his spiritual Fatherhood on the cross. Hence the Church's inebriated cry of Easter jubilation:

> O happy fault, O necessary sin of Adam,
> which gained for us so great a Redeemer!
> Father, how wonderful your care for us!
> How boundless your merciful love!
> To ransom a slave
> you gave away your Son.
>
> (From the Liturgy of the Easter Vigil)

Against the backdrop of what Jesus had to endure for Adam's fault, the liturgy's form of faith-expression is surely shocking, nearly excessive, almost cavalier. And yet it is none of these. For language itself strains to cope with the mystery of redemption. The 'O felix culpa' is as appropriate a response to divine mercy as linguistics will allow. The First Letter of St Peter indeed rivals the language of the liturgy in the way the writer there assesses the meaning of the cross. '[Christ] himself bore our sins in his body on the tree, that we might die to sin and live to righteousness. *By his wounds you have been healed*' (2:24). It is a reference to Isaiah's Suffering Servant again – '. . . wounded for our trangressions, bruised for our iniquities, upon him was the chastisement that made us whole; and with his stripes we are healed' (53:5).

The implications of this however are staggering. The wounds that bring us healing are the wounds caused by man's sin. That which destroyed our wholeness is the instrument by which wholeness is restored. The transgressions that ruptured

Christ's flesh are the means by which Christ's body, the Church, is cured of the scars of its own making. Through the indefatigable patience of God in Christ, through his ineffable power to draw good even out of evil, sin is expiated by sin!

The fourteenth-century English anchorite, Julian of Norwich, even understood the sins of the faithful to be the basis of their future glory. In her dialogue with God over a twenty-year period after the details of the passion had been revealed to her in vivid meditations, she came to see that iniquity once cleansed by the blood of Christ is not concealed in heaven as it is on earth. It is boasted of to the honour of God and of the transgressors. Moreover, that the saints of the kingdom are nothing other than sinners who discovered they were loved. Among those cited as examples are some of the most revered names of the Old and New Testaments.

> God also showed that sin will be no shame but an honour for man, for just as for every sin there is an answering pain in reality, so for every sin a bliss is given to the same soul. Just as different sins are punished by different pains according to their seriousness, so shall they be rewarded by different joys in heaven according to the pain and sorrow they have caused the soul on earth. For the soul that shall come to heaven is so precious to God, and the place itself is so glorious, that the goodness of God never allows the soul which will come there to sin without giving it a reward for suffering that sin. The sin suffered is made known without end, and the soul is blissfully restored by exceeding glories.
>
> In this sight my understanding was lifted up into heaven, and there God suggested to my mind David and

others without number in the Old Law. In the New Law
he brought to my mind first how Mary Magdalene, Peter,
Paul, Thomas of India, Jude, Saint John Beverley and
others, also without number, are known in the church on
earth with their sins, and how these sins are no shame to
them but have all been transformed to their glory. By this
honour, our courteous Lord shows for them here, in part,
something similar to what is done for them in fulness
there, for there the token of sin is transformed into glory.

*(Revelations of Divine Love)**

If the Jesus of Mark-Matthew's account says nothing of
this, utters no consoling assurance to sinners, it is because he
was inarticulate with agony, speechless with pain. The cross
itself however expressed his meaning adequately. It was a silent
soliloquy, the ultimate statement of his life, the most lucid
explanation of his ministry and mission as the Beloved
Servant, Beloved Son. The communities of Mark at Rome
and of Matthew in Syria recognised it as such. They were
conscious as they re-told the narrative that here was the sum-
mation of an existence so pleasing to his Father that no
sacrifice of the old dispensation could touch its efficacy for
atonement. All that went before pointed to this, awaited it,
not only in the Old Testament but in the daily life of Jesus
himself. Without Calvary, everything else Jesus did would
have been emptied of meaning. Good Friday completed the
significance of his words and actions, his teachings and healings, and verified their character as promises by delivering
what they promised at his death, and this 'not for the virtuous,
but for sinners' (Matt. 9:13).

The other reason why words were not needed from the cross

*Image Books, New York, 1977, Ch. 38, pp. 140–141.

is that Jesus had said it all to his disciples the evening before at the Last Supper. This was the Jewish Seder meal, the first of the days of Unleavened Bread, when God was blessed and thanked for the deliverance from Egypt and for the covenant. As Jesus took in his hands the loaf of bread – known from of old as the bread of affliction ('for you came out of the land of Egypt in hurried flight' [Deut. 16:3]) – he introduced a new element into the traditional rite. ' "Take, eat," ' he said to his disciples; ' "this is my body" '. Similarly with the wine: 'He took a cup, and when he had given thanks he gave it to them, saying, "Drink of it, all of you; for this is my blood of the (new) covenant, which is poured out for many for the forgiveness of sins." ' (Matt. 26:26–27)

In the Jewish mentality, to speak of one's body was to speak of one's very self. By giving himself as bread Jesus was recapitulating his wholehearted service to others as well as anticipating his final self-giving on Good Friday. As the disciples accepted the broken fragments they recalled how he had broken and given himself for three years in Galilee and Judea: long days spent teaching and preaching, feeding the multitudes, healing the sick, pardoning sinners; whole nights spent in prayer to the Father for those who had rejected him. They remembered the day he fell asleep in the boat, so exhausted that not even the storm awoke him. Neither could the sabbath precept interrupt his labour of love. When the Pharisees upbraided him for defiling the Law, he continued his work so undeterred that they plotted to destroy him.

As with the bread, so with the wine poured from the cup as his blood. For a Jew, blood meant life. Jesus had already poured out his life for the needy as a man pours a chalice to the dregs. He spared nothing of himself with blood, sweat and tears over the condition of the poor of Israel. Often his help was sought

67

by two people at once. Sometimes they brought all the ailing to him together. Frequently he had no time even to eat. In the opening chapter of Mark, the word 'immediately' is used nine times to underline the urgency with which he responded to all. On no occasion did he hold back from those in distress. Before the end of Passover week, that life would be literally poured out through the wounds of the cross, life-blood ebbing from his hands and feet upon a sinful earth. ' "Poured out for many for the forgiveness of sins," ' were the words he used – meaning by the Aramaic 'many' in fact 'all'.

The Passover context of this intimate Supper affirmed that the Paschal Mystery was a new deliverance: not from slavery in Egypt under Pharaoh, but from man's servitude to sin. The relation of the meal to the covenant identified Jesus himself as man's new relationship with God, the perfection and fulfil-ment of the bond forged through Moses after the exodus. That former alliance, once so promising, was now old and tired and anaemic. Here was new blood to give it life and youth and vitality, blood incomparably superior to that of the animal sacrifices which Moses drained into basins on Mount Sinai and threw over the congregation of Israel (Exod. 24:6–8).

As the meaning of the Supper revealed itself through its re-enactment 'day by day ... in their homes' (Acts 2:46), it acquired the status of liturgy for the brethren, became the focus of their identity as disciples and the binding force that united them. Sacred elements, sacred actions, sacred words became enshrined in a rite that is remarkably consistent in all the synoptics and St Paul. In the celebration of the Lord's Supper – the Breaking of Bread as it was sometimes called or the *agape* – the Church of the New Testament found the matrix of its faith-understanding of Jesus. The bread and wine, the breaking and pouring, the giving and receiving, the dominical words of institution, their symbolic meaning – provided a womb where the many disparate memories of Jesus converged, coalesced into an integral Memory of him as Messiah. Even more, the memorial meal had a sacramental capacity to draw believers into the mystery commemorated; it made them participators in the reality of salvation which Moses merely foreshadowed. Moses' covenant highlighted sin as a curse; in Jesus the curse was transformed into the blessing of redemption. His Supper made them recipients of that blessing.

Wherever Jesus is remembered in eucharistic sharing all his self-giving is rendered present again for sinners. Through the *anamnesis* his sacrifice bursts the banks of time and overflows into the here and now not in some spiritualistic, insubstantial manner but dynamically as forgiveness and reconciliation. What is remembered is neither some curious shard of history (interesting but anachronistic), nor an insufficient act that needs to be repeated. It is the perfect and eternal sacrifice which transcends created time, belongs to every era and is accessible to all men. When it is celebrated in faith it brings the past-historic into the continuous present to construct a future freed from the mistakes of both.

This was how St Paul envisioned it. 'As often as you eat this bread and drink the cup, you proclaim the Lord's death until he comes' (1 Cor. 11:26). By 'proclaim' he meant unleashing the power of the cross by one's faith-commitment to it. It was achieved by eating and drinking Christ's sacrificed form with gratitude and discernment: gratitude for the amnesty won by his suffering, and discernment of his ecclesial presence in the community that met to share his commemorative meal. Genuine thanksgiving would be exercised *through* genuine discernment, so that those who ate together would henceforth live for one another. They would understand that Christ must die in each so that he might live in all; that he must live in all so that they might die to themselves. In this way the Paschal Mystery would be perpetuated in his body the Church through all ages, extending his dynamic influence to the end.

When that death is thus re-called, proclaimed, celebrated, re-presented, it incarnates the Father's mercy in those who, re-producing the cross in their own lives, make the Beloved Son present in their midst. Participating in the sacrament of his passion they enter into communion with him and one another through the bread which is his flesh and the cup which is his blood. By that communion they identify themselves in terms of the breaking and pouring as he did. They actually *become* what they receive: ' "This at last," said the man (anticipating Christ and the Christian Mystery), "is bone of my bones, flesh of my flesh." ' (Gen. 2:23). Their union with Christ pledges them to carry his dying in their bodies for the sake of his body the Church. Their union with each other pledges them to share for his sake what he, their Head, endures in the lives of all. It is this openness to the cross that makes the Eucharist so meaningful an act, just as it is openness to the Eucharist that makes the cross so meaningful a way of life.

In the stillness of the Eucharist we understand what we failed to grasp in the silence of Calvary. Here the Father's voice explains the mystery of the cross in full. It is a 'still, small voice' that speaks, as the prophet Elijah discovered, carrying more force in it however than the earthquake, the great wind or the fire (1 Kings 19:12). It says that after Golgotha suffering does not erase human dignity; that just as sin, though a catastrophe, is no obstacle to growth once absorbed into Christ, neither is pain. Indeed when the crises of Christian living are inserted into the cross through the Eucharist, suffering enlarges the human spirit, matures the man, as does sin once repented of. Christ, after all, is still being crucified daily in the sinner as once he was crucified on the tree: yet as the cross was then the agent of anguish but is now the agent of salvation, so the sinner in dying with Christ and being buried with him becomes himself the instrument of grace. It is through suffering that he becomes so. This is why, far from diminishing one's nobility, endurance actually enhances it, especially when pain is accepted for the good of another.

Society today does not see it this way. Public debate on suffering betrays an attitude that is hostile to the gospel. The term 'mercy-killing' for example actually undermines the meaning of mercy by making a virtue of murder. Or consider the phrase, 'Death with dignity', so flippantly repeated now that one seldom stops to think about its sinister implications. Translated into the vulgate it reads, 'Euthanasia makes eminent sense'! Its subtle corollary is just as insidious: 'If you disagree, you lack *humanity*'. Equally dishonest is the invocation of 'freedom of choice' which ironically subverts real freedom by removing the issue from the sphere of moral responsibility. Finally, the appeal to 'quality of life' as a justification for opting to die is nothing less than a legitimisation of suicide, asserting as it does that quality over-rides the *value* of life.

It is a sobering fact that the more Christ's passion is rejected – in the elderly, the terminally ill, the handicapped, the unborn – the more death itself is idolised. But where Christ's death is accepted in all its anguish in his creature, there life is cherished and ennobled, people are loved in their dying, increase even as they decline.

This is what human beings really want: support to face the challenge of the cross. No one chooses to die. What they choose is not to be a burden on the unwilling. Behind the 'respectable' arguments for euthanasia they hear society's reluctance to share the suffering with them, which is what compassion actually means. They hear how much it costs to get personally involved in terms of physical and emotional energy, time, career and money. The polite but probing analysis of these costs in the media naturally arouses feelings of guilt in those who are no longer productive and are made to feel so. In such circumstances who would not prefer to be dead?

Quality of life is not commensurate with one's state of health. It has to do with being loved and appreciated. Nor is death with dignity the same as death without pain. It comes through being affirmed as a person even when one is losing everything. Only when one is stripped yet still treated with tenderness and respect does one believe in one's dignity. This was denied to Jesus. It is denied to him again in those who are allowed to plan their demise. In them Christ hangs silent a second time, desolate and dejected as before.

This is not to say that Christians are enamoured of suffering. For two millennia the Church has sought to alleviate pain in all its forms. It acts in imitation of Jesus who healed the sick and inaugurated the kingdom of God by doing so. In that kingdom the human person is regarded with the highest esteem, is elevated to share in the nature of God himself. This is why neither Jesus nor the Church ever mistook murder for therapy. Whoever believes in holiness believes in life, and whoever believes in life knows that sanctity is not divorced from suffering, but that each contributes something of its essence to the other in the wise plan of redemption.

Christ revealed the truth of this to his disciples from the moment he told them he himself must suffer. He put it in the form of a challenge that corrected their foolish notions of glory.

> 'You do not know what you are asking. Are you able to drink the cup that I drink, or to be baptized with the baptism with which I am baptized?' And they said to him, 'We are able'. And Jesus said to them, 'The cup that I drink you will drink; and with the baptism with which I am baptized, you will be baptized'. (Mark 10:38–39)

The cup was the cup of intense affliction. In the Old Testament it was generally thought to be reserved for the wicked, those destined in their sinfulness to drain God's wrath to the dregs. But in the New Testament it is the Holy One who is offered the chalice, the Man without sin who will empty it. In the Garden of Gethsemane the vision of that cup and all it entailed left Jesus prostrate on the ground, unmanned by its very prospect.

> Taking with him Peter and the two sons of Zebedee, Jesus began to be sorrowful and troubled. Then he said to them, 'My soul is very sorrowful, even to death; remain here and watch with me.' And going a little farther he fell on his face and prayed, 'My Father, if it be possible, let this cup pass from me; nevertheless, not as I will, but as you will.'
> (Matt. 26:37–39; Mark 14:33–36)

He made the plea no less than three times before he took hold of the cup and drank.

This was the same cup he had offered in sacrament to his friends an hour before. It was the cup of the covenant in his blood which they must consume as he did if they were to share in his work of sanctification. Not because they were sinners subject to punishment, but because they were disciples whom he had made holy. As they drank the communion-pledge with him at table, so they would drink what it signified in their own passion later. Even if at that moment they did not understand what they were doing (despite their words, 'We are able'), they would understand when the time came.

In the history of its martyrs and mystics the Church has always understood the necessity of suffering not in philosophical terms that win arguments but in experiencing it. There is a recognition that comes when one encounters the anguished, of a holiness beyond words, especially in the guiltless; an awareness of God's intense presence in the wretchedness of a soul that is utterly ravaged. In such cases prayer is the only feasible response. After such an experience it becomes very clear that the problem of pain, far from obstructing belief in a good God, actually increases it. Faith in God's Fatherhood is not only possible in the face of innocent suffering, it is positively required. Not to believe only creates more problems than it solves. Indeed, not to believe is somehow to deny and betray the innocent victim himself who in his desperation or acceptance of it all embodies what is perfectly good.

From the beginning there have been those whose commitment to Christ's imperative has been heroic. St Paul speaks in his Letter to the Galatians of bearing 'on my body the marks of Jesus' (6:17) – undoubtedly the first of the great stigmatists that would include Francis of Assisi and Padre Pio. For Paul these wounds were the credentials of his faith. 'Far be it from me to glory except in the cross of our Lord Jesus Christ, by which the world has been crucified to me, and I to the world. . . . I have been crucified with Christ; it is no longer I who live, but Christ who lives in me; and the life I now live in the flesh I live by faith in the Son of God, who loved me and gave himself for me' (Gal. 6:14; 2:20).

More remarkable still was the second-century martyr-bishop, Ignatius of Antioch. Outstanding among the hoards of early Christians who, while resigned to their deaths, went reluctantly, Ignatius actually longed for his fate. He is unique. In the letter sent to the brothers in Rome while still en route there by sea, he described his yearning for martyrdom in terms that have never been equalled.

> I am writing to all the churches and assuring them that I am truly in earnest about dying for God – if only you yourselves put no obstacles in the way. Pray leave me to be a meal for the beasts, for it is they who can provide my way to God. I am His wheat, ground fine by the lions' teeth to be made purest bread for Christ. Better still, incite the creatures to become a sepulchre for me; let them not leave the smallest scrap of my flesh, so that I need not be a burden to anyone after I fall asleep. When there is no trace of my body left for the world to see, then I shall truly be Jesus Christ's disciple.

> Even if I were to come and implore you in person, do not yield to my pleading; keep your compliance for this written entreaty instead. I am yearning for death with all the passion of a lover. Earthly longings have been crucified; in me there is left no spark of desire for mundane things, but only a murmur of living water that whispers within me, 'Come to the Father'. . . . I am fain for the bread of God, even the flesh of Jesus Christ; and for my drink I crave that Blood of His which is love imperishable.

> *(Epistle to the Romans,* §§ 4; 7)

Perhaps more impressive to the modern mind however is the witness of men and women who never sought suffering but embraced it fully when the good of someone else demanded it. One thinks of Maximilian Kolbe, the inmate at Auschwitz in 1941 who took the place of a fellow prisoner destined for the starvation bunker. Kolbe's triumph lay not simply in that he saved one man who eventually rejoined his family; nor that he gave courage and comfort to the other nine prisoners who died with him; not even that he himself perished without bitterness, co-operating with his executioner who injected the carbolic acid. It lay in the fact that in a hell-hole of unimaginable cruelty evil was conquered by goodness, hatred disarmed by love.

Without people like Kolbe we would despair of human nature because of the level of depravity to which it can sink. We would certainly despair at the grip evil has on mankind. But when the history of the twentieth century comes to be written it will have to acknowledge – in deference to the unsung saints whom Kolbe represents – that the race ascended to heights of glory much greater than the depths to which it descended, and proved itself capable of deeds that were truly supernatural, being the fruits of grace.

Had it not been for Christ's passion, that victory would be impossible.

If the martyrs prove the necessity of pain for loving God perfectly in others, the mystics likewise teach that suffering is necessary for loving God perfectly in himself. In this they touch the deeper significance of Jesus' words to those who would be his disciples. Golgotha is not simply the external battlefield where good and evil struggle in the interaction of the wicked and the just. It is more immediately the inner state of all human being in its pre-resurrection separation from God who is its source and destiny. What the martyr witnesses to (which is what 'martyr' means) is the agony of choosing what is right in preference to any consideration of personal convenience. His act is substantially a public one. The mystic does precisely the same but in a hidden way (which is what mysticism means), except that the object of his choice is the direct knowledge of God. Mystical communion with God through suffering transplants the very heart and soul of Calvary into the agonised consciousness of the contemplative. In his effort to renounce the self, in the anguish of knowing his incompleteness as a creature separated from his goal, he enters into the dark, contemplative agony of the Son on Calvary in his separateness from the Father as man.

Whereas the martyr bears testimony to the witness of Christ's love before the sinners who persecuted him, the mystic testifies to the Love which dared to be human as well as holy. For St John of the Cross it is this experience which constitutes perfection in the evolutionary journey of human being.

> At the moment of [Christ's] death He was certainly annihilated in His soul, without any consolation or relief, since the Father left Him that way in innermost aridity. . . . He was therefore compelled to cry out: 'My God, My God, why have You forsaken me?' (Mt. 27:46). This was the most extreme abandonment that He had suffered in His life. And by it He accomplished the most marvelous work of His whole life . . . the reconciliation and union of the human race with God through grace. The Lord achieved this at the moment in which He was most annihilated in all things: in His reputation before men, since in beholding Him die they mocked Him instead of

esteeming Him; in His human nature, by dying; and in spiritual help and consolation from His Father, for He was forsaken by His Father at that time so as to pay the debt fully and bring man into union with God. . . . [This was so] that the true spiritual person might realize that his union with God and the greatness of the work he accomplishes will be measured by his annihilation for God in . . . soul. When he is brought to nothing, the highest degree of humility, the spiritual union between his soul and God will be effected. This union is the most noble and sublime state attainable in this life. . . . [It consists] in the living, sensory and spiritual, exterior and interior death of the cross. (*The Ascent of Mount Carmel*, Bk 2, §11)

With Christ the mystic bears the full weight of his own humanity. He does so laying aside all the common illusions men indulge to disguise it. Purging himself of all that the self interposes between its own nothingness and God's fulness, he endures the devastating truth of his being-apart from the One who made him and who alone can make him complete. As the fourteenth-century author of the *Cloud of Unknowing* put it, the sorrow of the contemplative arises not from 'what he is' (namely a sinner), but '*that he is*'. In other words, that he is not yet totally immersed in God's perfection which is the deepest and ultimate desire of the human creature. 'When this sorrow is authentic it is full of reverent longing for God's salvation, for otherwise no human being could sustain it. . . . In a word, he feels the burden of himself so tragically that he no longer cares about himself if only he can love God' (Chapter 44).

In the writings of the twentieth-century mystic and visionary Sr Faustina Kowalska (1905–1938), the experience of abandonment is not only stunningly described in the clearest and simplest of terms; it is also explained. The dense trial of faith, hope and love, which reduces the victim to near-death is the necessary prelude to a vision of Divine Mercy. One is absorbed into that Mercy by sharing in the victimhood of the Crucified Redeemer. In the aftermath of the experience one is so transformed by the draining of Christ's cup that one becomes a kind of sacrament of compassion, an effective embodiment of the cross in the daily events and trials of life.

Faustina Kowalska's account of her premonition of the suffering she was to endure ends with the statement, 'My name is to be: "sacrifice" '. Her very identity was to be expressed and found in terms of affliction. Her innocence would make that ordeal efficacious for others. By her acquiesence – ('The Lord gave me to know that the whole mystery depended on . . . my free consent to the sacrifice') – the cross would be re-located in her, where she was, in what she did, in an extraordinary manner. The moment she gave her consent the dark cloud lifted and briefly she was shown the glory.

> At that moment, I realized I was entering into communion with the incomprehensible Majesty. . . . Then my spirit immersed itself in the Lord, and I said, 'Do with me as you please. . . .'
>
> Suddenly, when I had consented to the sacrifice with all my heart and will, God's presence pervaded me. My soul became immersed in God and was inundated with such happiness that I cannot put it in writing. . . . I felt that His Majesty was enveloping me. I was extraordinarily fused with God. I saw that God was well pleased with me and, reciprocally, my spirit drowned itself in Him. . . . And the Lord said to me, 'You are the delight of My Heart; from today on, every one of your acts, even the very smallest,

will be a delight to My eyes, whatever you do'. At that moment I felt transconsecrated. . . . God was now living in [my soul] with the totality of his delight. (*Divine Mercy in My Soul: The Diary*, Notebook 1, §§ 135–137)

Whether the visionary was aware of it or not she had just described, in the first person singular, the baptism of Jesus in the Jordan. The image she chooses to convey what she felt is that of plunging into water. Her repetition of 'immersed' for example draws attention to the idea from the start. The use of the word 'inundated' reinforces it. Then, 'my spirit *drowned* itself in Him'; the divine Presence 'pervaded me' (like a great wave); she was 'entering into' the incomprehensible Majesty (as into the ocean). As at the Jordan, God's voice resounds over the 'enveloping' of the mystic; his 'delight' with her is emphasised; she is 'transconsecrated' just as Jesus was anointed the Christ. The scene is a marvellous theophany, a spectacle of light and sound, a dramatic opening of heaven to earth – and at the same time the overture to sacrifice and pain.

She had glimpsed what St Paul saw in every Christian baptism: 'Do you not know that all of us who have been baptized into Christ Jesus were baptized into his death? We were buried therefore with him by baptism into death, so that as Christ was raised from the dead by the glory of the Father, we too might walk in newness of life' (Rom. 6:3–4). It is what scripture and the mystical tradition have always seen: the power and the glory and the suffering mixed; the power and the glory *in* the suffering; the kingdom emerging from the depths of the sacrifice.

It is this aspect of Jesus' baptism that Mark emphasises, and Matthew after him, in a Gospel where Jesus not only asks, 'Can you drink my cup?', but, 'Can you be baptized with the baptism with which I must be baptized?' In other words, can the disciple endure more than a passing trial, more than a single draught of bitter wine? Is he ready for a total immersion in the cross; for a change of identity in fact through the waters of life-long affliction? As Paul was – 'It is no longer I who live but Christ who lives in me' (Gal. 2:20), or Sr Faustina – 'My name is "sacrifice" '.

Whereas Luke self-consciously passes over the event of the baptism (merely noting it in the past tense and no more), and the Fourth Gospel omits it altogether, in Mark it provides the key to understanding Jesus as the Christ. Mark opens with the appearing of John the Baptist on the banks of the Jordan; this, properly speaking, is 'the beginning of the gospel of Jesus Christ, the Son of God' (1:1). It was, from after Pentecost, the starting-point of the apostles' preaching (Acts 10:37), a fact that undoubtedly influenced the first written version of the Good News.

The Jordan narrative, including the temptations, contains the entire passion and death proclamation in miniature. Hidden in symbolic language and imagery is the essence and meaning of the Paschal Mystery, the secret of Jesus' messianic identity and mission, his triumph over evil through commitment to the cross. It is told in covert fashion because that is how it was received. The truth is preserved in the telling yet the secret is maintained, to be unfolded gradually through the story of Jesus' life and crucifixion. A re-reading of his baptism after the passion will show the reader what he may have missed before: the clear mind and will of the Father at work in Jesus from the start. Then what was heard as whispers in the dark will be shouted from the house-tops with all the eager conviction of insight (Matt. 10:27).

In Matthew's elaboration of the Marcan source, even the question of Jesus' silence is dealt with at this primitive stage.

> Then Jesus came from Galilee to the Jordan to John, to be baptized by him. John would have prevented him, saying, 'I need to be baptized by you, and do you come to me?'
>
> (Matt. 3:13–14)

Implicit in the Baptist's reverent perplexity is the early Church's own effort to explain why the Lord accepted his fate with such holy quietism. Jesus' obscure reply – ' "Let it be so for now; for thus it is fitting for us to fulfil all righteousness" ' (3:15) – was pregnant with meaning for those who had ears to hear, who wanted to understand and be saved. At the same time it reflected the customary caution with which he guarded the nature of his identity from all but his most intimate associates. To grasp who he really was and what he had been sent to do would be to comprehend his silence immediately. It was to reveal these things that Mark structured his material with care.

On one level, the 'righteousness to be fulfilled' was that which any circumcised Jew subject to the Law would have wished to fulfil that day at the river. Through the Voice in the wilderness God was calling his people to spiritual renewal. No son of Abraham who had God in his heart could refuse that call. Especially not Jesus. The word he used to explain why he came – 'righteousness' – was the same he used later in his Sermon on the Mount. It indicated the kind of response the Father now required from the nation: a new and radical commitment of the heart, not the mean and measured strainings of its dutiful past. ' "For I tell you, unless your righteousness exceeds that of the scribes and Pharisees, you will never enter the kingdom of heaven". . . . "But seek first his kingdom and his righteousness, and all these things shall be yours as well" ' (Matt. 5:20; 6:33).

On a deeper level however the righteousness to be fulfilled could not be attained by John the Baptist's ministry for his was a call to repentance, not to justification. Neither could the Hebrew Law satisfy what was required, for it merely highlighted the sin that awaited forgiveness. Indeed, in the hands of the scribes and the Pharisees morality was reduced to sheer hypocrisy, as Jesus himself pointed out. In his own purity of heart he saw what was needed for his people: they could not enter into the kingdom unless the kingdom entered into them.

John's clarion call was Jesus' cue. The *kairos* moment had come. The Word recognised in the Voice his own summons from the Father to accomplish what the old dispensation could never fulfil: the inner cleansing of Israel and of the world. Water would not be enough for water removes only physical dirt. The precursor had said so himself as he acknowledged his own limitations. 'I baptize you with water for repentance, but he who is coming after me . . . he will baptize you with the Holy Spirit and with fire' (Matt. 3:11). Only by water and Spirit and fire and blood could the gold of humanity be refined, and only in a crucible so perfect that heaven itself must provide it.

At Jesus' baptism heavenly fire was plunged into the waters of the world. It set the seas aflame with grace. As in Egypt in Moses' time, the rivers were turned to blood – not that of God's curse but of his blessing in the Son whose life-stream imparted to water everywhere the efficacy of life. Rising up from the deluge of redemption that heavenly fire drew from its source the Spirit that created the first day and recreates the new day, spreading its healing light like sunset and dawn over earth and sky and sea. By fire and blood and water and Spirit the elements of the old creation are utterly annihilated, the new brought forth by an alchemy greater than creation-out-of-nothing, namely a re-creation-out-of-sin. Eden is re-populated. A new Adam has stood up. Soon a new Eve will emerge from his side. Together they will restore the rightful obedience due to the Father, crush the serpent's head as predicted, abolish the second death and instate the universal Israel in its promised inheritance. In Mark's account all the prophetic categories of deliverance are fulfilled in this opening of his Gospel which itself is fulfilled by Christ's death and resurrection at the end.

The writer of Mark was eminently familiar with the symbolic significance of water in the Old Testament as a figure of sin and destruction, of chaos. Early in his presentation of Jesus' ministry he recounts the calming of the storm at sea as a sign of Jesus' power not only over the natural order but over disruption in the moral order which confounds peace and leaves men exposed to fear.

> A great storm of wind arose, and the waves beat into the boat, so that the boat was already filling. But he was in the stern, asleep on the cushion; and they woke him and said to him, 'Teacher, do you not care if we perish?' And he awoke and rebuked the wind, and said to the sea, 'Peace! Be still!' And the wind ceased, and there was a great calm. He said to them, 'Why were you afraid? Have you no faith?' And they were filled with awe, and said to one another, 'Who then is this, that even wind and sea obey him?' (Mark 4:37–41)

From the very beginning of the Bible it required the Word of God and the Spirit of God to move across the face of the deep and into the darkness of the void to create order and calm

(Gen. 1:2–3). Later, when the intrusion and spread of sin is contemplated through the mythological stories of Genesis, return to chaos is depicted as the great flood from which only Noah and his family were saved. The Mark-Matthew tradition remembered how a dove over the dark water signalled the end of the catastrophe and the recession of the deluge. As God was pleased then to deliver his faithful and accept Noah's holocaust and make a new covenant, so under Moses he would split the waves of the Red Sea and rescue Israel from Pharaoh and from death. 'And the people of Israel went into the midst of the sea on dry ground, the waters being a wall to them on their right hand and on their left. . . . And Israel saw the Egyptians dead upon the sea-shore' (Exod. 14:22; 29–30).

In each case the story is one of life and death. It is one of life through death. And in each case God himself enters into the waters with his people. God and man together immersing themselves in all that the tide betokens – the depths of the human condition, its vulnerability, its need of cleansing, its mortality. Deliverance can never be by dispensation from the consequences of sin: justice is not served by overlooking injustice. Divine justice is satisfied by divine solidarity: God with his people, sharing with them the fruits of their sin that they might share with him the fruits of his saving power.

It is this profound and universal truth, trapped in the recurring imagery of scripture like marine-life under ice, that surfaces exposed in the melting reality of Jesus at the Jordan. His submersion in the murky flood-tide of the river as God's Son was the epitome of the divine solidarity in Israel's history. Here, in dramatic re-capitulation, was the mighty condescension of the incarnation; here, in ritual prefigurement, concealed in sign and yet revealed, was the humiliation of his passion and death. Not simply God and his people immersed

85

in the troubled waters of life on earth, but God *in* humanity without a foothold, drowning.

> Save me, O God,
> for the waters have risen to my neck.
>
> I have sunk into the mud of the deep
> and there is no foothold.
> I have entered the waters of the deep
> and the waves overwhelm me. (Ps. 68/69)

After Jordan the words of the psalmist apply equally to creature and Creator. As the Church intones the desperate sentiments expressed, it is hard pressed to decide whether the speaker is Christ or itself. In fact it is both in the same breath.

The moment Jesus accepted John's baptism for repentance he became enveloped in the polluted stream of mankind's sin. It encircled him, dragged him down in its turbid current and trailed him along the river-bed, depositing him in the rocky bowels of its tomb. In that instant Jesus identified himself as the Christ. Everything else that must happen would follow as a matter of course: his silence before his accusers, his acceptance of pain, the feeling of abandonment, his burial in the grave, his breaking of bread and pouring of wine, his ministry for others.

It was the moment of his public commitment to his mission, his crossing of the Rubicon, his day of priestly ordination. There would be no turning back from this. Son of God and Son of Man, he had given his pledge. He the Word, whose word was his bond, had given himself to the task. To renege would be to deny that very self for as God-made-man he was the bond between heaven and earth, the new covenant in whom the two were reconciled, united. As man, he vouched for mankind's new fidelity to God; as God he sealed the absolute and ancient fidelity of God's commitment to man. The horizontal and vertical dimensions of the covenant found their centre in him; intersecting, they formed the shape of the cross which centred itself on him. From the river Jordan he rose up *as* the cross, as the perfect alliance between earth and heaven, as the luminous rainbow spanning both, announcing the recession of the deluge and the appearance of the new world order of grace. The true Israel was emerging from its Red Sea, washed clean and set free for its desert journey to the spiritual Land of Promise.

In that instant the firmament melted to reveal the fulness of the Godhead.

> [Jesus] went up immediately from the water, and behold, the heavens were opened and he saw the Spirit of God descending like a dove, and alighting on him; and lo, a voice from heaven saying, 'This is my beloved Son, with whom I am well pleased'. (Matt. 3:16–17; Mark 1:10–11)

So perfect was Christ's action, its dramatic import, so moving the consecration of his will to the divine plan that in him man breached the impregnable gates of Paradise. Undoing Adam's disobedience he touched the Father's heart by his humility, compelled him out of his heaven to look again with pity on the race to which the Beloved belonged and to which he was passionately espoused.

The Spirit that rested on him with the meekness of a dove was the Spirit of the Father's tender heart going straight out to him. It anointed his humanity with all the strength of gentleness for his ministry of suffering, clothed him with power from on high to accomplish what he had been sent to do. By this holy anointing heaven confirmed Jesus as the

Christ, the One who was to come, the Lord's own Anointed, his Messiah – priest, prophet and king. No unction of the old dispensation ever made any man all three; the messiahs of the Old Testament were either priests or prophets or kings. Nor did their anointing bestow on them the fulness of the Spirit. The oil that sealed their status – like their status itself – merely prefigured the Oil of gladness with which Jesus would be sealed when he came. His priesthood would transcend theirs since his sacrifice was himself; his prophetic message would fulfil theirs since he was the Word he proclaimed from the cross; his kingship would surpass theirs since it was a reign of service and would last forever.

This anointing sacramentalised humanity. At Jesus' incarnation human nature had already been impregnated by the Word. Now it received also the Spirit. Spirit and Word together were thoroughly mixed into flesh, a healing salve of salt and oil rubbed into the putrid scars of sin. Henceforth all suffering would be messianic by association with the sufferings of Christ in corporate human form. Through that association all that was wounded would become whole. As St Cyril of Alexandria said in the fourth century:

> Christ is said to have received the Spirit, because he became man, and it was fitting for man to receive. Although he is the Son of the God and Father, and begotten of his substance even before the incarnation . . . he does not take it amiss to hear the God and Father address him after he became man: 'You are my Son; today I have begotten you'. [God says this] so that in [Christ] he may receive us into sonship; for the whole human nature is found in Christ, because he is man. Since the Father has

his own Spirit, he is said to give it again to the Son, so that in him we may gain the Spirit. . . .

The Only-begotten therefore receives the Holy Spirit not for himself; for the Spirit is his, and is given in him and through him; but because he was made man he had the whole nature in himself, that he might renew it all and restore its integrity.

(*Commentary on St John's Gospel*, Book 5, chapter 2)

The Lord's voice resounding over the waters echoes the significance of the Spirit's descent. It is a love-song full of affection for Jesus. More poetry than prose, it reminds us of the Song of Songs – 'Your name is oil poured out' (1:3): soothing oil on troubled waters, lavish goodness of God's own nature. In the sublimest form of human language it acknowledges that Jesus is divine, worthy of the Father's love for his own sake. At the same time it acknowledges the sublime nature of what he is come to do. As Son of Man he is worthy of the highest accolade from heaven for accepting the way of the cross. Here at last is a shepherd-Messiah after God's own heart (Jer. 3:15) who will gather into his perfect Sonship the scattered host of Child Israel. By his utter fidelity the Beloved will redeem the past and the future, compensating for the failures of both so completely that through him and in him all humanity will be God's one Beloved Son.

Looking down from above, the source of the Voice, looking down on the Jordan, looking down on the cross, sees what we from below looking up only partially see: the dignity of sacrifice, the poignancy of pain as an act of love, the efficacy of humility for rectifying the chaos caused by pride.

The Father's acclamation is more than the echo of poetry.

It is a direct quotation from the Servant's Song of Isaiah 42, first of the four prophetic predictions that Jesus completed.

> Behold my servant, whom I uphold,
> my chosen, in whom my soul delights;
> I have put my Spirit upon him,
> he will bring forth justice to the nations.
> He will not cry or lift up his voice,
> or make it heard in the street;
> a bruised reed he will not break,
> and a dimly burning wick he will not quench;
> he will faithfully bring forth justice.
> He will not fail or be discouraged
> till he has established justice in the earth;
> and the coastlands wait for his law. (vv. 1–4)

This is he who will take the trangressions of many upon himself and by his endurance make many to be righteous. Standing at the centre of history in the wash of the Jordan, on the hill of Calvary, he reinterprets pain. Embracing the agony of man – from the Unknown Servant of Isaiah's time to Maximilian Kolbe in ours – he raises even that which defeats us to the level of sanctity. He does so by absorbing it into himself and offering it to the Father. Hence all that was endured before him he now fulfils; all that must be endured after him, he fills.

Filling and fulfilling, the Son claims to himself the entire painful process of his body's growth to maturity. Leading the way as Head where all bodily pain is located, he lifts up his weak members with him, patiently bearing the stretch and stress of his limbs until they grow strong in him through the great parturition of the whole man. Watching, the Father observes the new birth of his Child and, despite the mucus and blood, marvels at what he has generated; observes too the first struggling steps, the development, the maturation, and like any father is 'well pleased' by what he sees.

No good parent would immunise his growing son from the experience of distress given the nature of reality. To do so would be to smother him at birth. The positive power of pain as a means to survival, in the building of character, in learning to cope, in attaining autonomy is universally accepted. If therefore one could re-create the world without suffering, one would not do so. The wisdom of God is reflected in the intelligence that acknowledges this. In Christ that wisdom attains its most sublime self-expression. As St Paul says, mirroring the mind of truth itself, 'I consider that the sufferings of this present time are not worth comparing with the glory that is to be revealed to us. . . . We ourselves, who have the first fruits of the Spirit, groan inwardly as we wait for adoption as sons, the redemption of our bodies. For in this hope we are saved' (Rom. 8:18–24). What the experience of life teaches on the lower level is thus confirmed by the Father's revelation of ultimate truth in the written word and the crucified Word, inspired by the Spirit of glory.

Nevertheless despite Paul's words the glory disappears in the Mark-Matthew tradition as the Jordan theophany ends. With stunning abruptness the river gives way to the desert: the trials of Jesus have begun.

Even divine commitment needs to be tested when enfleshed in the life of a man. The commitment of a human will too needs to be tried even when it is lodged in a divine Person. Was Jesus serious about the cross? Was he prepared to live out what the baptism ritual promised? Was he to be trusted unto death? No pledge, whether given by man to God or by God to men, is of value unless it is realised. Such is the nature of covenant: obligations must be kept by either side if the pact is to be profitable. In Jesus, God-made-man, the covenant which was embodied in him, which he Personified, was thoroughly tried and tested in every struggle of his human existence until it was shown to be flawless.

> 'If you are the Son of God, command these stones to become loaves of bread'. . . . 'If you are the Son of God, throw yourself down (from the pinnacle of the temple)'. . . . 'All (the kingdoms of the world and the glory of them) I will give you, if you will fall down and worship me', the devil said to him. (Matt. 4:3, 6, 8–9)

These were not three different temptations but the same one dressed in different guise. Avoid the way of suffering and choose another route to redeem the world! There are several more attractive methods of achieving the desired end. If Jesus wishes to establish a kingdom, what better way than to feed the poor, become a social reformer? Even better – if he wants to attract a following, why not bedazzle the crowds with his own goodness? He is, after all, Son of the Most High: let him then demonstrate his Highness from the peak of the Holy of Holies, prove his influence in high places, show his command of the supernatural powers of heaven to get things done. Or he could try the third way and ally to his cause the forces of evil. Providing he could stretch his conscience slightly, not be too scrupulous about it, he might make the end justify the means. By violence perhaps he could force his plans through, or by bribery, or lying, or blackmail or extortion. With intelligence and determination like his he could bring the world to its knees before him – maybe not in prayer but certainly in enforced servitude.

The suggestions of course were pure fantasy, as every temp-

tation is. Jesus saw through them at once and rejected them.
Only the cross gives access to reality. Yes, he *did* wish to feed
the hungry multitudes, but with food that would last. He
himself would become their Bread of Life but first the wheat
must be crushed, the grape trodden. Yes, he *did* want a following, but a community inspired by his love, freely assenting
to his graced friendship – not a mindless mass of superstitious
fanatics. And yes, he *did* envisage a universal reign, but one of
integrity and justice in spirit and truth – not an autocracy
founded on compromise with evil. Only suffering would
attract the response he wanted; only self-sacrifice would draw
that response from the ends of the earth and to the end of
time.

Although Matthew condenses the temptations into a single
chapter they did not end for Jesus in the desert. He took the
wilderness with him till he died. The same devilish alternative
shadowed him wherever he went: throughout his ministry, in
Gethsemane, even on Calvary! At each turn of the road he
repulsed it with the same simple fidelity by which he subju-
gated the human will within him to his divine will.

When Simon Peter tried to dissuade him from his course,
perceiving the darkness of Good Friday in Jesus' speech, Christ
rounded on him with unusual curtness: 'Get behind me, Satan!
You are a hindrance to me' (Matt. 17:23). It was the same
aspersory epithet with which he had dismissed the devil of the
desert. His commitment was not to be obstructed even by
the well-meaning.

To face the devil in a friend is one thing; it is quite another to
face him in one's own humanity. In the Garden of Gethsemane
Jesus, depressed to his soul, inundated by fears, submersed in
the grief of his immanent fate, overwhelmed by the prospect
of what he had undertaken, faced a threefold struggle with

himself that paralleled the assault at the start of his mission. True to the spirit of his Sonship he threw himself on the ground before his Father and prayed. When he rose to his feet to face the arrest it must have seemed that he had discarded his last opportunity to change his mind. Not so. The tempter that assails the weakness of man pursued his victim right to the end. While Jesus yet hung on the cross-beam, having conquered every insidious tactic of Satan, he could hear in the taunting remarks of the mocking throng, the very formula first used to waylay him in the wilderness of Judea.

> '*If you are the Son of God*, come down from the cross'. . . . 'He saved others; he cannot save himself. He is the King of Israel; let him come down now from the cross, and we will believe in him. He trusts in God; let God deliver him now, if he desires him; for he said, "I am the Son of God".'
> (Matt. 27:40–43)

It was the most incisive collation of all Satan's machinations ever recorded. Every element of his diabolical logic was included: the emphasis on the divine Sonship as power to manipulate; the disowning of the incarnation; the rejection of the cross (even at this late stage); the derisive scorn at his failure to survive, the impotence of his poverty of spirit, his kingship without a crown; the tantalising offer of Jewish faith on condition that he call a halt to his death; the absurdity of his trust in YHWH, and – worst of all – the soul-destroying implication that God had turned his back on him, had deserted him, no longer desired him. The silent voice of Satan had taken articulate form. What before was heard as a thought was now physically audible from the mouths of others. There was no shutting it out since there was no voice from heaven to over-ride it. At his very weakest, at the threshold of the portals of death, Christ could only listen and endure. But his final words to the empty universe leave no doubt that the abrasive speeches from below had etched their corrosive gall on the metal of his sensory soul.

In uttering those words – 'My God, my God, why have you forsaken me?' – the Son of God and Son of Man asserted the totality and therefore the perfection of his obedience to God and to Adam. At that instant the dead leapt for joy in the womb of the Underworld as the Father, speechless, received the sacrifice, too moved for words at the terrible beauty of his loving and Beloved Son.

Excursus:
Peter and the Passion

SIMON PETER, fisherman and disciple, viewed the cross
from two perspectives: from above and below, in accord
with the two aspects of his identity. As Cephas the Apostle
he recognised Jesus as the Christ. As Bar-Jona the fisherman
however he refused to acknowledge what that implied. He
followed Jesus willingly enough as his Messiah but retreated
just as quickly when he saw where that road was leading. In
this he epitomised the dual response to Jesus that the Mark-
Matthew tradition makes so much of: the faith of inspired
imagination on the one hand, the fear of a blind and stubborn
intellect on the other.

Paradoxically he symbolises both the opposition of the
Jews and the acceptance of the Gentiles. More than this, he
encapsulates the ambivalence even of the early Christians to
the message of Calvary. Hence he stands as a figure of many
believers today who, like him, profess faith in the crucifixion
while failing to follow it through.

This is why he is so great, the giant of the Mark-Matthew
drama, first among the Twelve, bedrock of the believing
Church, affectionately revered in every age by the weak and
sinful followers of the Petrine apostolic tradition. Great,
because he was precisely the material Jesus needed to lay the

foundation of a messianic community that would preach the redemptive power of failure. Pure granite in the eyes of that community too because in him the mysterious contradiction of the cross was solidly grounded. As the primitive gospel of the passion solidified in the telling, it necessarily preserved the geological fault in the Rock on which it was elevated. Simon Peter was living proof that when God is most rejected, betrayed and denied, God is most affirmed, proclaimed and believed.

The inconsistency of his character is laid bare at the very centre of Mark and Matthew's Gospels, at the very point where Jesus announces the inevitability of his suffering. It is clearly a matter of central importance to the narrative they have to tell. A discussion begins on the vital question of identity – that of Jesus, and of his followers. 'Who do men say that the Son of Man is?' Jesus inquires, 'Who do you say I am?' (Matt. 16:13–14). It is the most important question ever asked. Upon the answer depends the salvation of the world. 'Simon Peter replied, "You are the Christ, the Son of the living God" ' (Matt. 16:16). The answer is so precise, so spontaneous yet so full, that Jesus seems taken aback. The fisherman in his simplicity had drawn the two titles that perfectly describe Jesus and his mission: *Messiah*, and *Beloved Son*. Servant-Son of God. Startled, Jesus at once recognises in the other's confession, heaven's perception of him, not earth's. 'And Jesus answered him, "Blessed are you, Simon Bar-Jona! For flesh and blood has not revealed this to you, but my Father who is in heaven" ' (Matt. 16:17).

Because saving faith had been professed, a new identity had emerged among men. Simon Bar-Jona had touched the very heart, the very nature of the living Word. Like Moses at Horeb he had pronounced a sacred Name. Its articulation on his lips was to transform him utterly. Henceforth he would be known in terms of the Corner-stone he had unearthed and owned.

They were in the region of Caesarea Philippi. In the distance the triple-peaked Mount Hermon soared up to the sky, its eternal summit covered with perpetual snow. A veritable bastion of impregnable rock, its vast cliffs rose like the walls of a temple, immune to the ravages of time. 'And I tell you,' said Jesus, 'you are Peter [*Petros*], and on this rock [*petra*] I will build my church, and the powers of death shall not prevail against it' (Matt. 16:18).

In naming the Christ, the Beloved, Peter discovered his own new identity, his name of grace, his truest self. In that name was his vocation: what he was called to be, what he was to do. Upon his testimony others would know Christ in their turn, would find themselves, would construct communities of faith and salvation till the end of time. On his apostolic word the cross would be raised up for all to see, would be found worthy of belief, would be embraced.

How very ironic then that on Good Friday Peter, the Rock, was nowhere to be found. Like a stone falling through water he had quite simply vanished.

His unreliability was no surprise to Jesus. The incident at Caesarea Philippi forewarned Christ what to expect, for although Peter had accurately acclaimed the Messiah he had no idea what that really meant. Simon still harboured the illusion, as did most other Jews, of a military saviour who would deliver Israel from its political enemies, a champion like King David who would restore the kingdom of Judah to its former supremacy. Even when Jesus tried to explain the reality, to show 'that he must go to Jerusalem and suffer many things from the elders and chief priests and scribes, and be killed, and on the third day be raised' (Matt. 16:21), Simon Bar-Jona did not understand, did not want to listen. 'And Peter took him and began to rebuke him, saying "God forbid, Lord! This shall never happen to you" ' (Matt. 16:22).

In quick succession his words undid the faith he had voiced moments before. Now he saw the cross not from above but from man's point of view. The earthly part of his nature had obscured his heavenly vision. At once Jesus 'turned and said to Peter, "Get behind me, Satan!" ' (Matt. 16:23), thereby pronouncing the antithesis to Simon's name of grace, the untrue self, his non-identity: Satan, the tempter and father of lies who stands opposed to the Father of truth, the Father of the Beloved Son.

'Get behind me, Satan! You are a stumbling block to me; for you are not on the side of God, but of men.' A stumbling block, not a rock to lean on! A 'Hindrance' as opposed to 'Blessed are you'! Mere flesh and blood, of the earth, of sinful mankind, unsolid! The events of passion-week proved the unhappy prophecy true. Neither Mark nor Matthew attempted to soften the facts of his fall. He slept soundly in the Garden while Jesus wrestled with the chalice of affliction, drowsily succumbing to that same Passover wine which kept Jesus alert. At the Master's arrest, he 'forsook him and fled' (Matt. 26:56), while in the courtyard of the high priest he only 'followed him at a distance' (Matt. 26:58). Discipleship had been darkened by fear, apostleship eclipsed by apostasy.

Most degrading of all for this sturdy northern fisherman was that he denied the Lord for dread of a mere slip of a girl.

Now Peter was sitting outside in the courtyard. And a maid came up to him, and said, 'You also were with Jesus

99

the Galilean'. But he denied it before them all, saying, 'I do not know what you mean'. (Matt. 26:69–70)

The evangelist might have spared us the embarrassing detail, but he did not. His phrase, 'before them all', left Peter no place to hide. Mark made it even worse. In his account Peter's cowardice is embellished. 'I neither know nor understand what you mean' (14:68). But the girl had made no mistake: she had looked at him carefully by the light of the fire where Peter was warming himself.

Presently 'another maid saw him' and verified his identity once again, repeating and compounding his humiliation. By his second protestation he in fact demolished that identity, denied his own true self as well as the Christ. This time he did so with an oath. Finally it was the by-standers who reduced the Rock to rubble – nameless ones without a face, mere nobodies. Shamelessly 'he began to invoke a curse on himself and to swear, "I do not know the man" ' (Matt. 26:74). One wonders, as the cock crowed and Peter went out to weep bitterly, if his tears were not for wounded self-esteem as much as for infidelity to Christ.

One wonders also if Jesus' original name for him – Cephas, Petros, Rock-Upon-Which-I-Will-Build-My-Church – was not a cruel cynicism. Had it been anyone other than Jesus, we would be right. Simon's commitment, even after three years in Christ's company, was soft stone, mere tufa: the kind that can be scraped away quickly with the sharp edge of adversity.

Tufa however, though soft, is safe to live in. The Roman catacombs for example were scooped out of this volcanic residue in early Christian times. They formed a reliable network of honeycombed passages, layer upon layer running deeply underground, that provided refuge for the faithful in times of persecution. They have never collapsed in two thousand years. There, through the first three centuries, the Eucharist was celebrated in secret by many whose strength under trial was reinforced by the martyrdom of this same Peter. The designation of his new name was no vanity. As St Paul observed in his letters, God chooses what the world considers weak to confound the wise and the strong, so that it may be seen that the power belongs to God and not to us (1 Cor. 1:27; 2 Cor. 4:7). Indeed, like earthen vessels holding a rich spiritual treasure, the disciple of Christ must needs be fragile that his clay might be shattered. Only in this way can the fragrance of the resurrection escape to fill the entire house.

Christ chose Peter because he was fragile. He called him Rock not because he was unbreakable, but because he shared the vulnerability of the Corner-stone whose brokenness on Calvary would re-found the world. In pronouncing Simon's new identity, Jesus made him become what Jesus was himself. Not in the manner Peter expected but in a far better way: through defeat, disappointment, self-knowledge and utter dependence on God – all that Jesus himself experienced as man upon the cross.

Their partnership in pain was congruous with their partnership in the work of redemption. Matthew made this clear through a peculiar incident recorded only in his Gospel. Almost surrealist in its symbolism, it is placed after the story of Peter's confession of faith, and after Christ's second prediction of his passion. Peter is asked by the collectors of the Temple tax whether his Master pays the annual half-shekel. Its payment was incumbent upon every faithful Jew as a contribution towards the upkeep of the Jerusalem Sanctuary and its sacrificial worship – the thousands of rams and bulls for the burnt offerings, the vast quantities of incense and charcoal used in the repeated rites of expiation and atonement. Subscription entitled the Israelite to a share in all the blessings of the Law and the Covenant that were exclusively reserved for God's Chosen People.

Afterwards Peter and Jesus discuss the question in private.

> And when [Peter] came home, Jesus spoke to him first, saying, 'What do you think, Simon? From whom do the kings of the earth take toll or tribute? From their sons or from others?' And when he said, 'From others,' Jesus said to him, 'Then the sons are free'. (Matt. 17:25–26)

In other words, the Law of the Old Dispensation is for a nation of subjects – it does not make them sons. It keeps them under jurisdiction – it does not make them free. A different kind of tax was required to do that: the kind that only the Son could pay at the cost of his life. As Peter explained many years later to the newly-baptised of the Christian Diaspora in the First Letter attributed to him from Rome, 'Remember, the ransom that was paid to free you from the useless way of life your ancestors handed down was not paid in anything corruptible, neither in silver nor gold, but in the precious blood of a lamb without spot or stain, namely Christ' (1:18–19. JB).

These words were written shortly before Peter's own death by crucifixion in the stadium of Nero in AD 64. Perhaps, as he was led away to the same fate as his Lord, he remembered the strange end of that conversation with Jesus about the tax.

> [Jesus said to him], 'However, not to give offence to them, go to the sea and cast a hook, and take the first fish that comes up, and when you open its mouth you will find a shekel; take that and give it to them *for me and for yourself.*'
> (Matt. 17:27)

Two half-shekels from the mouth of the fish – early Christian symbol of the Messiah (*ICTHUS*: Jesus Christ, God's Son, Saviour). Jesus had sufficient resources to redeem all of them! His payment would cover Peter's apostasy in full (the half-shekel 'for yourself'), with enough left over to buy back the rest of humanity as well (the half-shekel 'for me') which Jesus had subsumed into his Sonship as man.

Furthermore, what Jesus would accomplish for the redemption of the world, Peter would be party to, would help him complete as his instrument. True, from the fish alone would come the reconciling atonement – from the word of its mouth, from the blood of its belly – but *Peter* would be the one to 'give it to them', to give it to the world through the Apostolic Church. Corner-stone and Founding-Rock together, this was to be an inseparable sign of salvation, a two-man net-hauling enterprise, a joint rounding-up of the flock, Head and hand of the Body in perfect synchrony extending grace to the ends of the earth. In and with Christ Crucified he found his maturest self, attained the fulness of his redeemed identity, of his personal vocation. Not through a power of his own but through the extraordinary power of Calvary working through his natural weakness. This was the message learned through bitter, salutary experience that he taught so convincingly to others.

> He is the living stone, rejected by men but chosen by God and precious to him; set yourselves close to him so that you too, the holy priesthood that offers the spiritual sacrifices which Jesus Christ has made acceptable to God, may be living stones making a spiritual house. As scripture says: See how I lay in Zion a precious cornerstone that I have

chosen and the man who rests his trust on it will not be disappointed. (1 Pet. 2:4–6)

If Simon Peter learned to lean his trust on the living stone rejected by men, it was not only because the cross taught him the cost of his sin. It was also because it taught him not to despair. The love that drove Christ to bear the brunt of Bar-Jona's apostasy was the thing that drew Peter's contrition. In one and the same movement Jesus' death revealed to the Apostle both his nothingness and his greatness. His nothingness, since he was in himself a weak, abject man. And his greatness, since it was for him that Christ died.

He understood therefore that what Jesus desired from him was repentance, not remorse. The former is the sign of real conversion of heart, the latter a symptom of inverted pride. Repentance allows one to look forward because one has left the past behind to the mercy of the Redeemer. Remorse forbids progress because it continually looks back, locking the spirit in fear. It is a malignant cancer that destroys the soul as it destroyed Judas in the Gospel, as it destroyed Lot's wife in the Old Testament. Disobeying the angel's message she turned to watch the destruction of Sodom and Gomorrah and was turned into a pillar of stone (Gen. 19:26), petrified! Simon on the other hand set his face to a future with Christ and became his Apostle, Peterfied! Calvary set him free, made him a son in the Son. Like St Paul, he could say, '[It is not] that I am already perfect; but I press on ... because Christ Jesus has made me his own.... Forgetting what lies behind and straining forward to what lies ahead, I press on toward the goal for the prize of the upward call of God in Christ Jesus. Let those of us who are mature be thus minded.' (Phil. 3:12–15)

Pressing forward, leaning on Christ, accepting his insufficiency, led Peter eventually to the highest form of faith: the will to suffer for Christ's sake. While Mark-Matthew does not tells us how Peter died, local tradition in Rome (still prevalent today) holds that he chose to be crucified upside down, deeming himself unworthy to be executed in the manner of Christ. Ironically he most clearly perceived the cross 'from above' when his head was closest to the ground in humility and poverty of spirit. His gaze was directed towards heaven only when his world turned head-over-heels. In that position his view of things finally righted itself. He saw reality as it was. There would be no more running away from truth, no further escape into fantasy. It had taken him a lifetime to reach his cross, to understand Christ, to know what it meant to be a Christian, to be broken like rock in a quarry.

According to legend he was still trying to avoid his fate only a short time before. Outside the walls of Rome, near the catacombs of San Callisto, stands a small church known as 'Quo Vadis'. It is said to mark the spot on the road south where Peter, fleeing from the persecution of the Christians after the great fire for which they were blamed, met the risen Lord coming towards him from the opposite direction. The Apostle stopped in his tracks. 'Quo vadis, Domine?' he asked, 'Where are you going, Lord?' 'Back to Rome', replied the Lord, 'to be crucified for you a second time.' It was where Peter should have been. He was after all leader of the community. Remembering his former apostasy, he turned and retraced his steps into the city to strengthen his flock and face his destiny.

The scene is depicted in fresco on the back wall of the sanctuary of the church. It is the first thing you see upon entering. Peter on one side, Christ on the other, facing one another on the road. The moment of encounter. A moment of truth. For the viewer the same challenge presents itself today.

Like Simon Bar-Jona, we believe that Jesus is God's Son, we
acknowledge all that happened to him. But his cross scandalises us, we avoid it as much as we can. Faith and unfaith, belief
and unbelief, acceptance and non-acceptance co-exist even in
the best. Intellectual recognition of Calvary does not always
reflect fidelity in the heart. This is shown by the fact of sin:
indifference, ingratitude, callousness, selfishness and pride –
all of it germinated by fear and cowardice. It manifests itself
most of all by a lack of care for those who suffer: the poor, the
sick, the marginalised. And yet even among the worst of us
there is always a spark of longing to be other than this, a daring
hope that at some time someone will recognise in us what
Jesus recognised in Simon Peter: a truer self, a potential *alter
Christus* capable of responding at a greater level than nature
allows. Someone who might draw out of us charismatically a
love by which we would transcend ourselves and the limitations we impose, or that are imposed upon us, from within
or without.

As you walk forward to inspect the fresco more closely in
'Quo Vadis', you become aware of two others painted on the
inside walls of the apse, left and right. Both are of a crucifixion.
The one is that of Jesus, upright, outside Jerusalem at Golgotha; the other, that of Peter, inverted, outside Rome on the
Vatican hill. Whatever mistakes Simon made as Bar-Jona, his
dying conviction as Cephas the Apostle was that

> if when you do right you suffer for it patiently, you have
> God's approval. For to this you have been called, because
> Christ suffered for you, leaving you an example, that you
> should follow in his steps. He committed no sin; no guile
> was found on his lips. When he was reviled, he did not
> revile in return; when he suffered he did not threaten; but

he trusted to him who judges justly. He himself bore our
sins in his body on the tree, that we might die to sin and
live to righteousness. By his wounds you have been healed.
(1 Pet. 2:20b–24)

The portrait of Peter presented by Mark-Matthew is one
that draws together all the themes implicit in their accounts of
Jesus' passion: the terrible effect of sin; the terrible mercy
of God; the terrible attraction towards suffering in the
repentant. But such a perception of Calvary needs to be
grounded in persons otherwise it remains only the Father's
perspective, above and beyond the reach of men's understanding. This is why the primitive gospel tradition dramatises
the impact of the cross in the Simon Peter sub-plot. The
passion of Peter runs like an undercurrent to the passion of
Christ, commenting on the main narrative, underscoring its
principal parts, highlighting its significant details, acting all
the time as counterpoint to the Song of the Suffering Servant.

Thus the Good News is embodied in the person of Peter, in
his moral suffering and his martyr's death, as it is embodied
in all who suffer penitently the effects of sin. It is personified in
them as the *kerygma* is personified in its preachers. Their
suffering is their proclamation of the gospel, their martyrdom
a witness to the credibility of the cross. This is particularly
true in those whose lack of bitterness or malice is such a
compelling sign of the kingdom. Their silence is so authoritative a testimony to pain's other dimension, so firm a
statement, it cannot be contradicted. Their vision of reality is
different from that of the world and yet so undeniably real in
itself, it forces us to reconsider suffering in the light of the
New Testament. We will know we view it in faith when we
find ourselves wishing to take pain away from another and to

107

bear it ourselves. Such an attitude is not logical, it is foolish. It only allows compassion to get the better of us. It is a perilous thing to let reason be seduced by love: this is what brought God down, un-throned him, made him utter out of pity a Word made flesh. If one were not careful one could become a piteous echo of that Word and be brought down too, could become another Beloved of the Father and then one's life would no longer be one's own. One would be unimaginably, frighteningly free.

If it happened to Simon the fisherman, it could literally happen to anyone.

CHAPTER THREE

'O My Beloved Father!'

The Lucan Passion Tradition

THE CRUCIFIXION as described by St Luke is a completely different *experience* for the reader who comes to it straight after Matthew and Mark. It is not that the writer is dealing with a different event or a different Jesus, but the way he handles his theme affects us differently. Whereas Mark-Matthew stresses the pain, Luke softens the impact. Mark-Matthew's Jesus remains silent; Luke's Christ articulates the meaning of the cross with an eloquence that inspires the reader with hope. And if the Messiah of the first tradition dies in an anguish close to despair, the Son of God in the Third Gospel breathes forth his soul with firm and confident trust in his Beloved Father.

One reason for the differences lies in the timing of the Gospels. Mark based his primitive version on a memory of Jesus' agony that was still fresh in the telling. It was written down in a climate of persecution. The early Christian foundations were staggering under Jewish aggression in Palestine and Asia Minor, and Nero's blood-letting in Rome. The passion of Christ was still throbbing in all the youthful members of his ecclesial body. The Marcan tradition bears the signs of the first numbing shock-reaction.

Luke's narrative on the other hand, written later in the

century, emerges from a period of reflection as the Church drew its second breath. By this stage Christianity was enjoying rapid expansion. Its preachers were beginning to see the fruits of their suffering. Their perception of the cross had had time to mature. They could perceive a relevance behind it that would not have been apparent before their trials. From their strong faith and tested courage Luke undoubtedly found not only his source material but also his positive and joyful tone as an evangelist.

But there is another reason too. Luke was, in St Paul's estimation of him, a 'beloved physician' (Col. 4:14), deeply sensitive to suffering, deeply committed to relieving it, one who recognised in Jesus' passion an inestimable power for healing. His proclamation of Jesus' death is vibrant with joyful hope. It marks the summit of his Gospel of the Gentle Saviour whose very Presence cured all manner of diseases, especially those associated with sin. Touched by the tender compassion of God's Son, Luke addressed his Good News first to the poor, the sad, the lonely, the desperate of the Gentile world who sought and failed to find understanding in their time. They lived in a society of pagans among whose worst vices, according to St Paul, were heartlessness and lack of pity (Rom. 1:31). Much like our world today.

To them and to us the Beloved Physician offers the immense consolation of a therapeutic Christ, a healing salve for a wounded universe. The stigmatised Son reveals not only God-with-us (Emmanuel), but also God-for-us. In the St Luke passion the God who shares man's lot is also a God who lifts us out of our misery, teaches us how to cope with it, and leads us shepherd-like through the mire to a new manifestation of God's kingdom on earth.

Luke's Calvary therefore is not the traumatised abattoir that is Matthew's Golgotha, but a hushed and hallowed place. No stunning of the dumb animal here, no savage slaughter of the defenceless beast, rather a serene and moving liturgy. Where one account is a dreadful dirge of inexpressible pity, the other is a *missa cantata*, a Schubert Mass in C. The first, a lament for the sin of the world; the second a celebration of forgiveness. Not to the exclusion of one by the other but in terms of narrative tone, and mood and colouring, the first is predominantly dark prior to the resurrection, the other shot through with a glory that makes the dying and rising one undivided, magnificent reality.

The tension of Gethsemane, for example, is significantly toned down in the Lucan tradition. Although Christ's sweat falls to the ground like drops of blood, he is comforted by an angel from heaven who strengthens him (22:43). The greater his agony, the more earnestly he prays. It does not lay him prostrate, he kneels. His petition is calm – 'Father, if you are willing, remove this cup' (22:42); not, 'If it is possible . . .', as in Matthew. There is no bitter rebuke of the sleeping disciples, no 'So, you could not watch with me one hour? . . . Are you still sleeping and taking your rest?' (Matt. 26:40, 45), and no triple rising from prayer to seek the solace that they did not give. Here, as in every instance where Jesus has an important decision to make, his prayer is noble and composed, a graceful preparation for the messianic task to which he is fully committed.

That same sedate composure marks the arrest and the road to Calvary. When the ear of the high priest's slave is sliced off by the sword of a disciple, 'Jesus said, "No more of this!" And he touched his ear and healed him' (22:50–51). The effect is one of reassuring calm in a magnetic field of agitation and panic.

On the way to execution, the Cyrenean forced to carry the *patibulum* follows behind, Jesus still leading the way of the cross as Lord. One thinks of a solemn liturgical procession. A great multitude follows him (unlike in Mark), both men and women: the Church. As in the first century, so till the end of time, Christ will always be Leader to glory of those who suffer with him and for him.

Women lament him: he is the classic noble hero, victorious even when vanquished, idealised by the wailing chorus of ancient Greek tragedy. He is not alone, is not left unmourned, he is not crushed. Already he is the 'Lord and Christ' of the Church's proclamation in the Acts, the 'Leader and Saviour', bearer of the name by which alone men may be saved (Acts 2:36; 5:31; 4:12). Luke's passion has all the grandeur, all the hall-marks, of epic-heroic poetry. Written to be read aloud it conforms to the great orations that eulogised the exploits of the mighty in valour, the immortal lords of war and peace who fought and defeated the foe even as they died.

This epic however is a spiritual one. Although in structure and style it made sense to the Greek-speaking world familiar with this genre, its immediate context is Jewish. Taken against Biblical heroic tradition which celebrated the saving deeds of YHWH, the Mighty One of Israel, it emits resonances of the cultic rites of enthronement in the Temple at Jerusalem. In Jesus' journey to Calvary one hears not just the voices of the crowd that formed his entourage, but a ghostly echo of the ancient tribes of Israel, songsters and musicians, that accompanied the Ark of the Covenant from Sinai to the Mount of Zion.

They see your solemn procession, O God,
    the procession of my God, of my king, to the sanctuary:

the singers in the forefront, the musicians coming last,
between them, maidens sounding their timbrels.

(Ps. 67/68)

The cause of jubilation is the sense of security YHWH provides for his people. His coming home to them in the Land he
gave them is the culmination of his works of deliverance. His
presence in their midst, focal point of true worship, is their
guarantee of his continued protection. 'Father of the orphan,
defender of the widow, / Such is God in his holy place' (v. 5).
So complete is his victory on their behalf – ('The Almighty
has defeated a numberless army / and kings and armies are in
flight, in flight': vv. 11–12) – that he can afford to be generous
to his foes.

You have gone up on high; you have taken captives,
receiving men in tribute, O God,
even those who rebel, into your dwelling, O Lord.

(v.18)

Thus even the Lord's enemies are fortunate. Their captivity is
a privilege that allows them to enjoy his beatific Presence.

What gives this Jewish epic cosmic significance is that
YHWH's sphere of influence extends beyond Israel to include
all nations. He who makes the earth to tremble, causes the
heavens to melt, who thunders his mighty voice, whose might
is in the skies, is One to whom all peoples will come, drawn by
his splendour and glory.

For the sake of your temple high in Jerusalem
may kings come to you bringing their tribute.
Kingdoms of the earth, sing to God, praise the Lord. . . .
Come, acknowledge the power of God.
[Because] he bears our burdens, God our Saviour.

113

This God of ours is a God who saves.

(vv.29, 32, 34, 19–20)

In the Jesus epic all the elements of greatness are fully incorporated which appear as incomplete realities in the epic types before him, sacred or profane: the tragic charisma of the Greek young-god; the grandeur of 'Elohim; nobility of character, triumph of purpose, the rout of the ignoble, the cosmic acclaim. But in this case the reality signified is turned inside-out and back-to-front – the very opposite of what we expected to see.

Jesus is not only non-violent in his greatness, he is submissive as well. His prowess is pure gentleness, his strategy compassion; he actually prays for his persecutors.

> And when they came to the place which is called The Skull, there they crucified him, and the criminals, one on the right and one on the left. And Jesus said, 'Father, forgive them; for they know not what they do.'
>
> (23:33–34)

His words are repeated again and again. Not apparent perhaps in translation, this becomes clear in the original Greek where the imperfect tense is used. Literally, 'Jesus *kept saying* [these words]' all the time the nails were being driven into the wood.

Most stunning of all in this incident (exclusive to Luke), is the quality of that prayer and its timing. It occurs at the very moment of crucifixion. To forgive one's friends is one thing; to pardon one's enemies, given time, is not impossible either: time is a great healer. But Christ's forgiveness was instantaneous. Time did not heal this offence, Jesus did. Beseeching his Father's mercy he even went so far as to make excuses for his killers – 'They know not what they do' – and when no

114

excuse was possible, he absolved them. Mercy absorbed him, not pain. Pain usually kills any desire other than its own relief. He however was preoccupied with reconciliation. The idea possessed his mind entirely. It was his obsession.

For Pope St Gregory the Great, the irony of redemption becomes apparent when we measure Christ's docility against the Bible's outrage at the murder by Cain of his brother Abel.

> What purer kind of prayer can be cited or imagined than that which consists of merciful intercession for those who are the cause of the pain one is suffering? So it came about that our Redeemer's persecutors eventually drank as believers the blood which they had spilled in their rage, and proclaimed that he was the Son of God. . . . The blood of Jesus speaks more graciously than that of Abel because Abel's blood sought the death of the brother who killed him, but the blood of the Lord won life for his persecutors.
> (*Commentary on the Book of Job*, Bk. 13)

Luke was deeply impressed by this ultimate sign of the cross: its victory over the evil that caused it. In the Acts – sequel to his Gospel – Jesus' readiness to excuse is duplicated in the patience of the Church which extends his reconciliation through time and space. So when Calvary is re-produced in the death of Stephen for example, the young man repeats Jesus' dying words even as he is being martyred. 'And as they were stoning Stephen, he prayed, "Lord Jesus, receive my spirit." And he knelt down and cried with a loud voice, "Lord, do not hold this sin against them" ' (7:59–60).

As before, so also now: the waves of hatred break their strength on innocence, humility, unconditional forgiveness. A truth emerges: evil is self-destructive when confronted by love's gentle acquiescence. The conversion of Saul, the other young man standing by who approved Stephen's murder and witnessed Calvary in it, proved the point. As Paul the Apostle he not only continued Stephen's mission of proclaiming Christ and verifying the gospel with signs and wonders. He did so on a scale and with an effect that Stephen could never have accomplished given the difference in their personalities and talents.

Jesus' readiness to excuse was part of the Church's early preaching too. When Peter addresses the Jews in Solomon's Portico after the healing of the lame man, he concludes his condemnation of the killing of Jesus with the words: 'And now, brethren, I know that you acted in ignorance, as did also your rulers' (3:17). An amazing extenuation, given that, as he stated himself in his case for the prosecution, 'you delivered (Jesus) up and denied him in the presence of Pilate, when he had decided to release him ... you denied the Holy and Righteous One, and asked for a murderer to be granted to you, and killed the Author of life' (3:13–15).

The same allowance is made for the Jews in Paul's kerygmatic speech at Antioch of Pisidia. Detailing the Old Testament texts of the history of salvation which paved the way for the coming of Christ, he pleads diminished responsibility on the part of those in Jerusalem who rejected Jesus and their rulers, 'because they did not recognize him nor understand the utterances of the prophets which are read every sabbath' (13:27). The argument is so spurious in the light of what they did to Christ, it would never stand up in a court of law. But the balance of mercy is tilted in favour of the unjust: that is Luke's point as he structures the speech for Theophilus.

Even the pagans benefit from the same generous accommodation. Although God gives to all men life and breath and

everything, Paul announces to the Athenians at the Areo-
pagus, and even though their own poets acknowledged that
'we are indeed his offspring' so that they *ought* to have known
better than to worship images of silver and stone, nevertheless
'the times of ignorance God overlooked' (17:30).

Jew and Gentile alike therefore enjoy the latitude of Christ's
graciousness on the cross. It comes easily from him because of
who he is. In Jesus, as Shakespeare wrote,

> The quality of mercy is not strain'd;
> It droppeth as the gentle rain from heaven
> Upon the place beneath: it is twice bless'd;
> It blesseth him that gives and him that takes.
> 'Tis mightiest in the mightiest. . . .
> It is an attribute to God himself,
> And earthly power doth then show likest God's
> When mercy seasons justice. Therefore, Jew,
> Though justice be thy plea, consider this,
> That in the course of justice none of us
> Should see salvation: we do pray for mercy,
> And that same prayer doth teach us all to render
> the deeds of mercy.
>
> (*The Merchant of Venice*, Act IV, sc.i, 182–200)

Mercy was not strained in Christ. It flowed. In him justice was
fully seasoned with compassion – so seasoned that the two are
forever indistinguishable: Christ's merciful compassion is true
justice, is *justification* for sinners. No further justification is
needed before the court of heaven. His prayer from the cross
over-rides judgement, surpasses it.

His mercy is twice a blessing too. It blesses Christ as God
who bestows forgiveness from the cross. It blesses him again
as man, who receives his own forgiveness on behalf of all. Thus

Christ's sufferings are to him, as God-made-man, a double glory: in him God and man are mutually glorified, each blessing the other as salvation and thanksgiving are simultaneously exchanged through the one action of his passion.

Christ is the Sacrament of divine compassion just as the Church is the sacrament of Christ. This is the over-all vision of Luke-Acts, the evangelist's two-volume work. It explains why Luke draws attention not to the brutality of Calvary, but to its effects. The beating that left Christ's body all tender manifests the tenderness of the divine heart. The thorns and nails that opened raw wounds expose the unseen substance of the Father's sincerity. The tolerance of the Father in heaven is fleshed out in all that Jesus tolerated on earth; his long-suffering patience proven in the prolonged suffering of the Son; his passionate kindliness in the agonised passion of his Progeny. Christ aglow with pain *is* God's painstaking care, writ large in illuminated manuscript.

It was surely the St Luke passion that prompted one of St Peter Chrysologus' famous sermons on the spirituality of Romans 12, for Luke was Paul's travel-companion and imbibed much of Paul's perspective on Christ.

> God wants to be loved rather than feared. . . . He does not want to be so much the Lord as a father. God makes a request in his mercy, rather than punish in his severity.
>
> Listen to what the Lord asks: 'You see in me your body, your limbs, your organs, your bones, your blood. If you are afraid of what belongs to God, why do you not love what is your own? If you run away from your Lord, why do you not run back to your kinsman?
>
> 'Perhaps you are ashamed because of the greatness of the passion which you inflicted on me. Do not be afraid.

This cross is not mine; it is the sting of death. These nails do not pierce me with pain; they pierce me more deeply with love of you. These wounds do not draw groans from me; rather they draw you into my heart. The stretching-out of my body makes room for you in my heart; it does not increase my pain. My blood is not lost to me; it is paid in advance for your ransom.

Come then, come back to me, and come to know me as a father; for see, I return good for evil, love for injuries, and for deep wounds a deeper love.' (Sermon 108)

In this passage, is it God who speaks, or Christ? The term 'Lord' is applicable to either. Yet the interchange of 'my body', 'my wounds', 'my heart', with the words, 'Come to know me as a father', suggests a kinetic fusion of two Persons so that it is difficult to distinguish between the speaker and his speech. A fusion, but not a confusion – such is Peter Chrysologus' intention, such was Paul's and such was St Luke's. The mind and mildness of the Father is perfectly translated in the crucifixion of the Son. God's winning approachability unmistakably spelt out in the approachability of Christ: in his courteous words, his benevolent patterns of behaviour, in his body language on the cross.

His arms for example were stretched out wide on the *patibulum* to the right and to the left: the gesture of an embrace that extended to the utmost points of the compass, drawing the whole world into his heart. No one was to feel excluded. Nailed wrists made the gesture permanent. It would never come undone because this was the Father's covenant-promise to men. The remarkable Psalm 102/103 had already made the assurance in words; now it is seen in flesh. 'As far as the east is from the west/so far does he remove our sins.' To read the idea in verse is comforting; to watch it literally come true on the cross is awesome. Christ measuring in mime the remove of man's sin!

'For as the heavens are high above the earth', continues the Psalm, 'so strong is his love for those who fear him'. The east-west direction of the cross is complemented by its north-south dimension. Jesus united earth and heaven with his whole body, racked and strained to form a bridge for men to walk on, a ladder for men to climb to God. Such was the strength of YHWH's love. But what imagination would have dared interpret the psalmist's belief so radically? The body language of the cross defies the hesitating modesty of faith's expectations. It derides the reluctance to believe that mercy is infinite.

Christ crucified does not simply state that God is compassionate. He proclaims that God is *compassion*. North, south, east and west, the limbs of Christ's frame radiate the very nature of the Deity. The Father cannot but show mercy because mercy is of his essence. Extraordinarily the psalmist had grasped the truth many centuries before, but who had even heard him? 'The Lord *is* compassion and love.' Therefore,

> it is he who forgives all your guilt,
> who heals every one of your ills,
> who redeems your life from the grave,
> who crowns you with love and compassion. . . .
>
> He does not treat us according to our sins
> nor repay us according to our faults. . . .
>
> As a father has compassion on his sons,
> the Lord has pity on those who fear him. . . .
> [For] the love of the Lord is everlasting . . .

and his kingdom is ruling over all.

(Ps. 102/103)

To say that the Lord is compassion, to state that God is love, is the furthest language can go in identifying the Divine. And yet it falls short of letting us know him. What, after all, is compassion? What is love? An invisible concept until we meet it in a one-to-one relationship. This is what the Christ of St Luke achieves. This is what it means to call Christ a Sacrament.

The sacraments are outward signs of a hidden reality; they make visible by signification the grace that is actually working God's salvation within the life of the person who receives them. To observe the sign is to experience the reality that brings about a change. Christ and the Father are as close as the outward sign (the *sacramentum*) is with the reality of grace (the *res*). Together they are one. *Sacramentum et res.* Therefore to see and believe what is happening on Calvary is to come face to face with salvation.

But a sacrament is more than a sign. It is an efficacious action that delivers what it signifies. Christ's death is not just a good omen of things to come, an icon of mercy. It confers mercy in the eternal 'now' of God's saving Presence to us. Consequently to encounter Christ is to encounter the Father. Knowledge of the Crucified Son is knowledge of God. What is compassion now? No longer merely an idea. It is the Person of the Son. He is all compassion. Hence he is God's fullest definition, God's identity.

This being so we meet God in pain as well, because pain is a kind of sacrament of the passion, particularly in the baptised. God engages his people in the suffering of life as he engages them in the sacraments of the Church. The Son enfolds the anguished in the embrace of the cross just as the Father enfolds the Son in accepting his sacrifice. This is why Calvary is for Luke a cause of celebration, a celebration in itself.

It explains too why pain in the Third Gospel is always a type of liturgical experience. When the sick are brought into contact with Christ, they are so transformed that their sickness becomes a means of communion with the Godhead. What they experience is the infinite solicitude of the Father burning tenderly in the gentle eyes of his Son. The effect is a sudden release of joy. It is the same in the post-Pentecost Church where his influence reaches the maimed, the lame and the possessed through the ministry of the Apostles. Luke-Acts abounds with one-line descriptions of the people praising God, giving glory, expressing delight, rendering thanks. And the pattern is still spiritually imprinted on the Church's liturgies today where the sick assemble to celebrate the cross: at a Eucharist for healing, a service of Anointing, or a communal Rite of Penance before Easter.

All the patterns of compassion in Luke culminate in his handling of Jesus' reaction to the Good Thief. The Healing Christ tradition peaks at this point, revealing the theological purpose of the passion narrative as, itself, the culmination of Jesus' ministry of mercy. Here Christ's deepest care for the salvation of the poor is localised in his care for the man dying with him. The grace of the crucifixion is not meant for some amorphous mass of anonymous humanity: it is aimed at each individual human being, however undistinguished.

Moreover this grace goes beyond the temporal healing of mind or body that so often prefigured it. Jesus is not merely – like Luke – a good physician. He is the Saviour. What he promises is not just a brief respite from present ills but an immediate and permanent remedy for the basic disturbance at the root of human being. What he guarantees is not only what is requested – remembrance when he comes in his kingly power, but even more – Paradise 'today' (Luke 23:42–43).

The Good Thief's agony ended in his death. His pain did not go away until it ran its course. Yet he died in peace, accepting what he described himself as 'the due reward of our deeds' (23:41). In the humility of self-knowledge he was able to turn to Christ and ask for what he did not deserve. This is the real healing that the Father accomplishes through the Sacrament of his Son on Calvary. The Thief's last thoughts were for Christ. You and I, he reminded the other thief, are under condemnation justly, 'but this man has done nothing wrong' (23:40–41). The gentle innocence of the Saviour had moved him. His own experience of crucifixion (imposed against his will) sensitised him to the poignancy of Jesus' fate, so willingly accepted. What the episode shows is that suffering *evokes* compassion, and that compassion produces *repentance*. Thus the cross heals the spirit of man, making him human again, giving him back the humanity he had lost through pride and lack of pity.

This is what the Old Testament prophets tried to accomplish when they demanded *metanoia* in Israel, a change of heart. They failed because they did not have access in their preaching to the cross. The best they could do was prepare the people for Calvary. Genuine sorrow is never requisitioned on demand. It is drawn out of the heart that hears love calling in the cry of love's victim. Jesus is God's prophetic love-call which human nature cannot ignore. His desire to be loved in return, freely, has a forcefulness more compelling than anything the old dispensation could produce. The prophet Zechariah, for example, could only speak in the future tense of the kind of response God required.

> On that day . . . I will pour out on the house of David
> and the inhabitants of Jerusalem a spirit of compassion and
> supplication so that, when they look on him whom they
> have pierced, they shall mourn for him, as one mourns for
> an only child, and weep bitterly over him as one weeps
> over a first-born. (12:10)

In Luke's Calvary this text is fulfilled. Not just in the response
of the Good Thief, but in the spontaneous lament of the
crowds at Jesus' death and in the sombre tone of the centurion.

> Now when the centurion saw what had taken place, he
> praised God, and said, 'Certainly this man was innocent!'
> And all the multitudes who assembled to see the sight,
> when they saw what had taken place, returned home
> beating their breasts. (Luke 23:47–48)

Repentance is never too late. Jesus' demise did not render their
sorrow redundant. It was precisely for this that he died. In
him, the new Prophet, God was able to bring about what no
prophet before could possibly have done: a removal of the
barriers to conversion. In this sense the crucifixion was a
double fulfilment of prophecy. Not only did Jesus complete
the future predictions that were made about him; he also
completed the very function of prophecy itself as a ministry of
summoning God's people back to their covenant with the
Father.

Just as Christ's mercy was not strained, neither was the
crowd's contrition on Good Friday. Once barriers are removed
it is natural for people to respond positively to pain. Grace
working on nature at Calvary perfected the penitence of those
who witnessed the death. The beating of the breast, the
acknowledgement of Christ's innocence, the subdued praising

of God signified that all the defences had come down. Hardness of heart had given way in a vision of God that was disarmingly different from any they had ever been taught.

When one suffers for another as Jesus did, it forges a bond that the sufferer is not likely to break. So much of the self is invested in what has been endured that to lose the other would be like losing oneself: one thinks of a mother with her child after giving birth, or comrades in war who have risked their lives for each other. To look upon the dead Christ and know that this is how God feels towards men, is to know we are worthy of a lasting love.

As soon as that fact lands and explodes in the imagination, the human person is conquered. Not by a blitz on the free will – for that is always left intact – but by voluntary capitulation. Like one who is irresistibly attracted towards something that is perfectly good and decides he must have it. In our life this is what changes us: to find we are important when we thought we were not; to be surprised by forgiveness when we expected condemnation; to realise we are understood after bracing ourselves for judgement.

At Calvary all bollards collapse that once protected us from the negative effects of insecurity, guilt and fear; the bollards of gross self-assertion, bitterness, feigned apathy and coldness towards others which obstruct *metanoia*. The result is a kind of self-transcendence, self-forgetfulness: a reckless disregard for our rights (real or imagined), for our projected image, for our addiction to success, and a joyful loss of interest in all our previous obsessions.

It was to this end that the preaching of the cross was directed in the Acts. The proclamation of Calvary always leads to the call to conversion. At the end of Peter's Pentecost Sermon the crowds 'when they heard this were cut to the

125

heart, and said to Peter and the rest of the apostles, "Brethren, what shall we do?" And Peter said to them, "Repent, and be baptized every one of you in the name of Jesus Christ" ' (2:37–38). Throughout the work Luke scatters short summary-verses that repeat over and over how the Church grew in numbers as that call was heard and received. The compassion of the Gentle Saviour was conquering the world by setting it free.

An incident recorded early in the Third Gospel illustrates the way Christ's gentleness worked towards effecting repentance. Jesus is dining with Simon the Pharisee when a woman of bad reputation, a prostitute, enters the house and approaches him. Kneeling at his feet she washes them with her tears, dries them with her hair, then kisses them and anoints them with ointment. The language is so frank, the action so intimate, it is actually slightly embarrassing. The Pharisee indeed was shocked. This woman had become reckless, oblivious to her image, unconcerned about convention. Whatever she had been in the past she was now a lover of Christ, uninhibited in the expression of her feelings because her love was holy.

Jesus was neither ruffled nor put out by her behaviour. On the contrary he was profoundly impressed. He recognised repentance at once. He understood that here the Father had already pardoned all. Since God's forgiveness comes through the Son, this woman could only have obtained grace through her contact with him. She had evidently observed the kind of man he was, and believed.

The other evangelists place a narrative similar to this closer to the event of the cross, portraying the woman's anointing as a preparation of Jesus' body for burial. Luke deliberately re-positions the story in the context of Christ's public life, undoubtedly to show the connection between the two. Just as the anointing before his passion in Matthew, Mark and John indicated faith in the sacrifice he was about to make, so in Luke's Gospel that anointing – coming earlier than it should – recognised the mercy of the cross already at work in the compassion that marked everything he did and taught.

The woman who wept for him and for her sins at the house of the Pharisee had watched Jesus' delicacy with the sick, his kindness to sinners, his concern for the down-trodden; she saw what the others saw on Good Friday. This was a humble and joyful man, a very attractive Person. He had a way of making you feel good, he brought goodness out of you; he brought happiness with him, he refreshed you. She found herself changed just by being in his company. When he spoke she recognised a God she could believe in, a spirituality that made sense because it believed in people, in their dignity, in their potential, and was not dismayed by their failures. It was a realistic message that breathed hope in those who had got lost in the various ways that people do. Jesus made her see that she could go home again to her Father.

Under the warmth of such acceptance, love blossomed. Jesus recognised this too. ' "Do you see this woman?" he said to Simon, "I tell you, her sins, which were many, are forgiven, for she loved much; (for) he who is forgiven little, loves little." And he said to her, "Your sins are forgiven. . . . Your faith has saved you; go in peace" ' (Luke 7:47–48). She had been caught up in the cycle of grace that unites the Father with his Beloved Son and draws others through its centripetal force straight to the heart of salvation: mercy bringing forgiveness, forgiveness inspiring repentance, repentance evoking love, and love confirming forgiveness.

What makes the story rich and worth telling is the extravagance of the woman's reaction to Jesus. It was not necessary to do what she did. A simple word of thanks would have sufficed for the mercy God had shown her. It could have been conveyed in private without fuss. Others did, like the woman with the haemorrhage who slipped up behind him in a crowd for healing and then tried to slip away again, or Nicodemus in St John's Gospel who visited Jesus by night. The prostitute however chose to show her gratitude in public and did so in the most ostentatious way imaginable.

Obviously her manner reflected sincerity of feeling. But Luke had another reason for telling it the way he did. The mercy of God is an extravaganza of tenderness. He is lavish with loving-kindness, irresponsibly forgiving, a reckless prodigal with his gifts of grace, unstinting in heart-felt compassion. As Jesus said in tribute to his Father's generosity, urging his followers to be the same:

> Be compassionate as your Father is compassionate. Do not judge and you will not be judged yourselves; do not condemn, and you will not be condemned yourselves; grant pardon, and you will be pardoned. Give, and there will be gifts for you: a full measure, pressed down, shaken together, and running over, will be poured into your lap; because the amount you measure out is the amount you will be given back. (Luke 6:36–38)

Such opulence deserves to be made public. It requires more than passing acknowledgement. If the exuberance of mercy is met with a tame response, it dilutes the effect of God's goodness and its point, which is repentance. Good news needs to be announced with vigour and hearty acclaim otherwise it ceases to be good news and the opportunity it affords passes by.

It was the extravagance of God's goodness to the lost that Jesus tried to communicate in the parables that appear only in Luke. The incarnation was living proof of an extravagantly loving God, but even when people are faced with such proof in the flesh words are still needed to explain it to them. Such was the purpose of the stories of the Shepherd with the hundred sheep (though this one appears in Matthew, it draws a different conclusion), the Woman who lost a drachma, and the tale of the Prodigal Son.

These parables were prompted by the jealous murmuring of the scribes and Pharisees who noted that tax collectors and sinners were gathering around Jesus and drawing towards him. They were scandalised that he received them and even ate with them. To justify his welcoming attitude he said to them, 'What man of you, having a hundred sheep, if he has lost one of them, does not leave the ninety-nine in the wilderness, and go after the one which is lost, until he finds it?' (Luke 15:3–4).

Objectively the question is an odd one. No responsible shepherd would leave a flock in the wilderness just to retrieve a wanderer. It would be foolish to do so. Sometimes we have to cut our losses. If the write-off is small we can live with it. But not this shepherd. 'And when he has found it', continued Jesus, 'he lays it on his shoulders, rejoicing. And when he comes home, he calls together his friends and neighbours, saying to them, "Rejoice with me, for I have found my sheep that was lost" ' (vv. 5–6).

The situation now is not only foolish; it is downright ridiculous. The scribes and Pharisees might well have regarded Jesus with some suspicion and exasperation. But Christ was not talking about shepherds and sheep any more. He was speaking about God's pastoral concern for the individual. 'Just so, I tell you, there will be more joy in heaven over one sinner who

repents than over ninety-nine righteous who need no repentance' (v. 7). The Pharisees would have stiffened here. Did he
mean them? Was he referring to the self-righteous? Was
he accusing them at the cost of justifying reprobates? In the
light of the whole gospel, especially the crucifixion, he was
doing just that!

The Shepherd story makes its impact by gross exaggeration.
It is because the man's solicitude for the one stray is so extreme
that he is a marvellous model of the compassionate God. Not
only in his going off to search for the sheep, but in his idiotic
joy at finding it. He carries it on his shoulders. He calls in
neighbours and friends. He throws a party! One wonders if he
was in his right senses. Such is the sensibility of the God who
sent his Beloved Son to be the Good Shepherd of men.
What Jesus rescued was not even profitable sheep but the
unprofitable bestiality of infected human nature. It was this he
carried on his shoulders by taking humanity on himself and
carrying it as a cross. And did so with rejoicing, calling the
nations together in celebration.

The extravagance of divine love is confirmed by the still
grosser exaggeration of the parable of the missing drachma.
The housewife's loss represented a mere ten per cent of her
housekeeping finances. Nevertheless she conducts a search,
even though it is night, that turns her home upside down.
'What woman, having ten silver coins, if she loses one coin,
does not light a lamp and sweep the house and seek diligently
until she finds it? And when she has found it, she calls together
her friends and neighbours, saying, "Rejoice with me, for I
have found the coin which I had lost" ' (vv. 8–9).

Once again the example is framed as a question that
demands a response. This time the hypothesis is even more
ludicrous than before. Whatever might be said for a shepherd

seeking sheep, the distress of a wife over a coin defies compre-
hension. Even if one accepts that she was poor, or that her
budget was stretched, or her household unusually large,
nothing accounts for her hosting an open-house for her friends
when she found it. The cost of such hospitality would easily
exceed the drachma recovered! Her over-played enthusiasm,
like that of her neighbour the shepherd, is strangely at odds
with the loss and recoup involved.

Yet small things are important to women, just as sinners are
important to God. Housewives are punctilious by nature; they
care about details that no one else would notice. Similarly the
heavenly Father cares about the loss and recovery of the outcast
and forgotten. Though his assets are not enlarged by the
finding, he cannot rest until his due returns to him. The cost
of redeeming the insignificant might well outweigh the deficit,
but that does not matter. He pays it willingly, wastefully,
wildly, with exuberant satisfaction. 'Just so, I tell you, there is
more joy before the angels of God over one sinner who repents'
(v. 10).

The parables are not meant to confound the economist.
Luke is making a serious point about hope. After Christ, no
one is too impoverished to be of value to God. Consider
the one stray sheep, says the evangelist, think of the lost
drachma, and you begin to understand the Father of Jesus:
more jealous than a herdsman, more meticulous than a
housewife.

Hence Luke's tales are deliberately laced with light-hearted
humour. Their purpose is to make the sinner laugh. Laughter
undercuts the seriousness of the sinful situation, as forgiveness undercuts the seriousness of the human condition. The
humour of the gospel highlights the anomaly of despair. With
the coming of Christ hopelessness is no longer an appropriate

response to evil. The Son's death so completely restored what was lost that the balance of credit is magnificently redressed. After such a recompense to be without hope when one has repented is simply ridiculous.

It is the function of humour to expose untruth wherever it dresses itself up as reality. By contrasting real truth with its monstrous imitation the gentle humorist forces his audience to recognise the fantasy of sin in their lives and correct it. In making them laugh at themselves, he succeeds in making them humble. By making the laughter gentle, he succeeds in giving them hope. Only those who refuse to change cannot laugh. Why should they indeed? There is nothing for *them* to laugh about. Their situation is irremediable. The Pharisees belonged to such as these. They were staunchly entrenched in their self-justification. Since they were not prepared to alter they dared not laugh with Jesus, so they laughed *at* him, scornfully. It was their most serious defect.

For the rest, merriment is proof of faith in God. Those who trust him have no difficulty in laughing – at themselves, at human imperfection, at mortality. All these things are recapitulated in Christ, are trodden under his feet so that God's creature might be restored to the original harmony the Father always intended. Joy therefore is a sign of holiness. It signifies deliverance from the depressing power of darkness. It affirms the complete victory of Christ's cross and is itself, according to St Paul, one of the hallmarks of the Holy Spirit (Gal. 5:22). Joyful laughter is a hymn in praise of the redemption. It surges up from the heart that overflows with freedom, that recognises the kingdom of God within itself. It cannot but cry out, it cannot be surpressed, it is a gift of tongues.

The prelude to the Third Gospel resounds with such music in Mary's Magnificat, her joyful song in praise of God her

Saviour. It is based on the thanksgiving prayer of Hannah in
the Old Testament at the conception of Samuel. This woman's
faith was so self-expressive she was accused by Eli the priest of
being a drunkard. Like her uninhibited style of praying, her
words of gratitude do nothing to hide her spiritual intoxi-
cation.

> My heart exults in the Lord,
> I find my strength in my God;
> my mouth laughs at my enemies
> as I rejoice in your saving help.
>
> (1 Sam. 2:1. GV)

Though equally controlled, Mary's Canticle bears the same
inner freedom as Hannah's song, echoes its exuberance, comes
close to breaking the Jewish protocol of sober self-restraint in
God's Presence.

> My soul glorifies the Lord,
> my spirit rejoices in God, my Saviour.
> He looks on his servant in her lowliness;
> henceforth all ages will call me blessed.
>
> The Almighty works marvels for me.
> . Holy is his name!
> His mercy is from age to age,
> on those who fear him.
>
> He puts forth his arm in strength
> and scatters the proud-hearted.
> He casts the mighty from their thrones
> and raises the lowly.
>
> (Luke 1:46–52. GV)

133

In daring to laugh at God's enemies the Mother of Christ, like the mother of Samuel before her, declares the mercy of God superior in the contest against evil. She had good grounds for such confidence. She could feel that mercy stirring within her as the Child of her womb.

Her fertile laughter joins with that of all who placed their hope in the divine promises of the Old Testament. The incredulous laughter of Abraham, father of Hebrew faith, and his wife Sarah, with which the history of salvation began: 'Then Abraham fell on his face and laughed, and said to himself, "Shall a child be born to a man who is a hundred years old? Shall Sarah, who is ninety years old, bear a child?". . . . And Sarah, listening at the tent door behind him, laughed to herself, saying, "After I have grown old, and my husband is old, shall I have pleasure?" ' (Gen. 17:17; 18:10, 12). Or the revelry of King David who danced before the Ark as it was borne into Jerusalem, and defended his lack of inhibition to his mortified wife in terms of his dependence on God:

> Michal the daughter of Saul came out to meet David, and said, 'How the king of Israel honoured himself today, uncovering himself today before the eyes of his servants' maids, as one of the vulgar fellows shamelessly uncovers himself!' And David said to Michal, 'It was before the Lord, who chose me above your father, and above all his house, to appoint me as prince over Israel, the people of the Lord – and I will make merry before the Lord. I will make myself yet more contemptible than this, and I will be abased in your eyes'. . . . And Michal the daughter of Saul had no child to the day of her death. (2 Sam. 6:20–23)

The moral of the Hebrew scriptures was clear. Sarah and Hannah, though old or barren, bear children but Michal does not; Abraham and David father the multitude of Israel. Those whose faith knows how to laugh before God give life; those whose haughty dourness betrays a faith gone dry, remain sterile. Luke's Infancy Narrative verifies the truth of ancient wisdom and brings it to fulfilment. Though Mary is unmarried and virginal, her humble trust fills her womb with Life itself. She is a sign to all who wait in joyful expectation of God's deliverance.

Not surprisingly her spiritual Canticle ends with reference to Abraham, returning full circle to the beginning of the Promise. It affirms the eternal gyration of mercy that catches in the fulness of grace all faith's children to the end of time.

> He protects Israel, his servant,
> remembering his mercy,
> the mercy promised to our fathers,
> to Abraham and his sons forever.
>
> (Luke 1:54–55. GV)

The Abraham of Genesis and the Mary of Luke: twin pillars of ecstatic fidelity to God's word. Upon them rests the great edifice of the plan of salvation. For St Luke, Mary is the new Abraham in whom the incredible dream of her forefather came true of a progeny as many as the stars of heaven – the Church; and of a land of milk and honey – the messianic kingdom of grace. Her fresh and vigorous virginal faith renews the youth of Abraham's ancient spirit. Her courageous joy proclaims her father's faith fulfilled. In her Magnificat the whole gospel is fully contained and announced, albeit in embryo, that same gospel which the Patriarch believed and saw in its infancy (Gal. 3:8; Heb. 11:13; John 8:56).

When her kinswoman Elizabeth hears the rapture of Good News in the Virgin's voice, she is transported. Elation thrills

135

the very core of her who, despite advanced age, is herself already six months pregnant.

> And when Elizabeth heard the greeting of Mary, the babe leaped in her womb; and Elizabeth was filled with the Holy Spirit and she exclaimed with a loud cry, 'Blessed are you among women, and blessed is the fruit of your womb!. . . . For behold, when the voice of your greeting came to my ears, the babe in my womb leaped for joy. And blessed is she who believed that there would be a fulfilment of what was spoken to her from the Lord.' (Luke 1:41–45)

Such is the effect of the message of mercy. It makes the child within the human soul exult, the soul of the remnant of Israel, grown elderly under the suffering of centuries and the weight of man's primeval sin, yet heavily pregnant with expectant faith in God's sworn saving help.

As man Jesus knew what it was to feel this joy that was Israel's hope. In the passage where he praises his Father for revealing these things to mere babes but keeping them hidden from the learned and clever, Luke prefaces Matthew's text with the line which is purely Luke's own: 'In that same hour [Jesus] rejoiced in the Holy Spirit and said, "I thank thee, Father . . ." ' (10:21). One feels the same well-spring of gladness bubbling up from the mind and heart of Christ that characterises every page of the Third Gospel. Emanating from the Father in the Spirit through the Son, it splashes over like water on to the dry soil of parched human longing, irrigating the tired spirit of mankind. For ' "no one knows who the Son is except the Father" (continues Luke's passage), "or who the Father is except the Son and any one to whom the Son chooses to reveal him" ' (10:22).

In revealing the Father to men Christ used the full range of his good-natured wit to show the ease with which God might be petitioned in time of need. A love of banter was part of his Personal charm. If this was how the Father revealed the Son and the Son the Father, men indeed might well relax in the divine Presence. For wit is the ultimate means of dissolving distance. It is therefore the kindest form of mercy. Addressing a group of men with their children in his audience, he puts it to them, ' "what father among you, if his son asks for bread, will give him a stone; or if he asks for a fish, will instead of a fish give him a serpent; or if he asks for an egg, will give him a scorpion?" ' (Luke 11:11–12). None of the men present could have resisted a guffaw, nor could Jesus' tone have been other than sparring. Jewish fathers did not need to be taught how to love their offspring. By the same token, neither does God. ' "If you then, who are evil, know how to give good gifts to your children, how much more will the heavenly Father give the Holy Spirit to those who ask him!" ' (11:13).

The gentleness of his jocularity shows that Jesus knew that men are children too. Before the Almighty they are afraid, self-conscious, as children are. Nervous, vulnerable, dependent. Not always in control of the forces that mould them, uncertain how to cope. Ask! urges Jesus, search! knock! You will be given, you will find, doors will open! Men and children together will know God as Father because they have known Christ as Brother and recognised themselves in him, in his humour, his wit, his accommodating Personality. Divine mercy had shaped itself into the sparkling eye of a teller of unusual tales. Like Son like Father. A God who would speak so personably to inspire confidence, what lengths might he not go to, to fulfil that confidence?

The last tale of the three in Luke 15 was to answer that question definitively. The story of the Prodigal Son is *the*

Parable of Paternal Tenderness, the parable of parables. It is the perfect prelude to the cross, the ultimate preparation for the passion. After hearing this no audience that had really listened could further question the compassionate nature of Jesus' God. And especially after Calvary, when the tale was re-told in the light of his death, none could have doubted that Calvary was the parable translated into the common language of pain that all understand. Luke's Prodigal Son was no fairy-tale. It was literally true, but in a way that at first escaped notice for its full import was half-hidden by its own irony.

The parable climaxes with the celebratory feast in honour of the Prodigal's homecoming. It is a truly extravagant affair. The sound of the music and dancing is so pronounced that it carries over the fields and into the distance. Superlatives are used in the instructions given to the servants.

> The father said to his servants, 'Bring quickly the best robe, and put it on him; and put a ring on his hand, and shoes on his feet; and bring the fatted calf and kill it, and let us eat and make merry; for this my son was dead, and is alive again; he was lost, and is found. And they began to make merry. (vv. 22–24)

Every detail is itemised in the organisation of this banquet: the apparel, the menu, the music. Exquisite care is taken to get it right. The planning is both spontaneous and elaborate. The feast begins without delay. All this indicates a disposition on the father's part that is conciliatory beyond words and irrevocable. His delight at his son's return is so instantaneous, it was obviously what he longed for most.

The party spirit emanating from the house is reminiscent of the soirée hosted by the wife who found her drachma, or the shepherds' get-together, except on a grander scale. One supposes from the text that the old man joined in the dancing and singing himself – 'Let us eat and make merry', he said, and the other son was able to hear 'music *and dancing*' as he drew near to his home. The implication in Jesus' story is that God so exults at the sinner's repentance that he dances as David did before the Ark. The thought is a daring one and yet the metaphorical nature of the parable allows it. A daring thought, but not without precedent.

The seventh-century Old Testament prophet Zephaniah, preparing his people for Israel's crucifixion – (the Babylonian Exile, less than half a century away, was to bring the nation to near-annihilation) – concludes his prophecy with the promise of reconstitution. The Exiles will return, he says; humbled and chastened, they will be restored. YHWH himself will bring them home, a Mighty Warrior in their midst, and no one will dance more rapturously than he:

> Shout for joy, daughter of Zion,
> Israel, shout aloud!
> Rejoice, exult with all your heart,
> daughter of Jerusalem!
> Yahweh has repealed your sentence;
> he has driven your enemies away. . . .
> He will exult with joy over you,
> he will renew you by his love;
> he will dance with shouts of joy for you
> as on a day of festival.
>
> (3:14–15; 17–18. JB)

St John Damascene used the term 'dancing' – *perichoresis*, translated as *circumincessio* in Latin – to describe the relationship and interaction of the three Persons of the Trinity. The idea conveys perfect partnership, perfect synchrony, perfect harmony of heart and mind and will among Persons who, though distinct and individual, are uniquely One. While this is not the intention of the Old Testament prophet, nor even Luke's intention in the New Testament, these texts of revelation are not at odds with the revealed nature of forgiveness and reconciliation. The dance is eminently suited as a paradigm of the Godhead's openness to others, a Godhead who is by nature himself a Communion. The dance of the Trinity therefore is an *in*clusive and not *ex*clusive state of being, acting and loving. It invites participation in the divine life, encourages and welcomes all to join in and become one. For since he created man in his own image, he did not intend for man to dance alone. The measure of God's absolute perfection in fact is his absolute wish to share freely what he enjoys fully within himself.

The dance is equally a paradigm of man's return to God. It idealises the intimacy restored by reconciliation, the graced fellowship that follows forgiveness. It typifies the sheer joy of coming together again, being as it is the traditional symbol of celebration, of family reunions, Christmas and Thanksgiving, weddings and nuptials, where dancing expresses the concord and solidarity of the paternal home. But even more, the image is liturgically significant, dance being part of the ancient ritual of covenant renewal. The rhythmic wholeness of being back in step with God again, the freedom of faith's physical expression, the exhilaration of now yielding, now advancing in time with the Other – all this presenting in human form the profound mystery of God's mercy and love. It was for the dance that he created, that he redeemed, that he continues to sanctify his chosen partners, his beloved sons. Similarly it is for the dance that men are called to repent, to laugh and rejoice, to worship.

The celebration of the Prodigal's return peaks with the slaughter of the fatted calf. It was a wild over-reaction to the boy's re-appearance. His apostasy had been wilful – not just a slip of youthful weakness. He had deliberately demanded all he could take and left for a life of debauchery. Moreover he came back only because the money ran out and he was hungry. He figured he could do better for himself at home. His return therefore was no less selfish than his departure. While one might understand a father's willingness to put the past behind and say no more, what is astonishing is the way this father pandered to the youth and humoured him. He was more prodigal with his love than the boy was with his fortune.

And yet, ironically, the reality to which this refers is more astonishing still. For it was no fatted animal the heavenly Father slaughtered to celebrate the return of profligate mankind. It was his Beloved Son.

To look again at the Salvador Dali Crucifixion and see the suspended Christ, not this time as bull's head of the Temple sacrifices, but as the skulled remains of the Prodigal's banquet, is to meet the mystery of the Father's compassion in Luke. It is to differentiate the Christian concept of mercy from its Hebrew prefigurement which pales in comparison. Indeed every model of mercy pales when set against the reality, even those in the parables. The exaggerated extravagance of the homing shepherd shouldering his sheep, the euphoric house-wife arranging her party, and indeed the father's slaughter of the fatted calf, fall short of the crucifixion of Jesus. Though the scriptures do their best to prepare us, there is no radium-protection against the Good News of Calvary because the compassion it proclaims is infinite.

If the celebratory banquets in the parables seem wasteful, unnecessary, since their cost exceeded the loss recovered, how much more is this true of Christ's death. And yet it *was* necessary in the Father's plan to save his other children. The risen Lord affirms this twice in Luke's account of the resurrection appearance on the road to Emmaus:

> And he said to [the disciples], 'O foolish men, and slow of heart to believe all that the prophets have spoken! Was it not necessary that the Christ should suffer these things and enter into his glory?' And beginning with Moses and all the prophets, he interpreted to them in all the scriptures the things concerning himself. . . .
>
> Then he said to them, 'These are my words which I spoke to you, while I was still with you, that everything written about me in the law of Moses and the prophets and the psalms must be fulfilled.' Then he opened their minds to understand the scriptures, and said to them, 'Thus it is written, that the Christ should suffer and on the third day rise from the dead, and that repentance and forgiveness of sins should be preached in his name to all nations, beginning from Jerusalem.' (24: 25–27; 44–47)

Astounding words from the mouth of the victim-Son himself: it is not the Lord of the gospel who is foolish; it is *we* who are foolish, for not realising that God's love is as mysterious as it is real. The effect of those words on his hearers was prophetic – 'Did not our hearts burn within us while he talked to us on the road, while he opened to us the scriptures?' (v. 32); 'And they worshipped him, and returned . . . with great joy, and were continually . . . blessing God' (v. 52). It would be sustained in the Church's grateful response to the St Luke passion in every age, wherever men should seek the reassurance of divine gentleness towards the sinner.

The extraordinary profligacy of the fatted calf however does require some kind of rationale, since the parables are not irrational; God's mercy is not without reason. Theologically the calf is not the only Christ-type in the story as Good News. The Prodigal himself is a figure of Jesus. The sin-burdened son, ascending to his father's house, pronouncing words of contrition, begging reconciliation, seeking re-admittance, humbling himself, content to be no more than a hired servant – all of this as much befits Christ as the character in the parable. The fact that the character-type was guilty while Jesus was not, in no way diminishes the likeness. Indeed it enhances by contrast the reality of the God who took upon himself the sin that belonged to us. When that same God, now represented by the Prodigal's father, accepted the contrite humanity that came back to him from Calvary he welcomed home his own divine Likeness, his heart's delight. For such a One a fatted calf is no extravagance.

And insofar as the body of that repentant Child whom he embraced in the flesh was the frail, weak Church in its sinful members, the cross was no extravagance either. Though emaciated on account of sin, the Church is still his poor Son's body. For such a One, what ransom is too high to pay out in redemption? Thus the Beloved Son died for the Beloved Son when Jesus died. That is why tenderness in excess is easily imparted to us from above: we are Christ with Christ in the Father's heart. So integral is God's love that the One Son slaughtered brought the same Son home, the same Son sacrificed celebrates the One Son's return.

The medieval theologian, Blessed Isaac of Stella, saw the logic of the cross in the fact that the human and divine natures were perfectly conjoined in the compassionate Jesus.

He bore on the cross in his human body all the sins of the

whole body; and by the grace of rebirth he has granted to his spiritual body that it shall be charged with no sin. For scripture says: 'Blessed is the man whom the Lord has not charged with his sin.' That blessed man is clearly Christ; insofar as God is his head, Christ forgives sins; insofar as the head of the body is one man, there is no sin to forgive; but insofar as the body of the head is many men, there is sin, but it is not charged.

He is righteous in himself, and makes himself righteous. He is the one Saviour, the one saved. . . . [He] takes away the sins of the world which he bore, who is priest and sacrifice and God, who offered himself to himself, and so through himself reconciled himself to himself, as well as to the Father and the Holy Spirit. (Sermon 42)

The structure of Luke's parable provides the sacramental pattern of salvation in the life of the Church. First conversion, then communion. First the return, then the repast. The Prodigal's repentance, then the meal. It is the structure of the Eucharist as celebration of compassion. First the broken-hearted, then the broken bread. The same pattern was adopted by the Church from the beginning. In Luke's Acts the newly baptised converts are described as 'dedicated . . . to the apostles' teaching and fellowship, to the breaking of bread and the prayers' (2:42). The penitence expressed by their baptism is followed by the nourishment of word and sacrament. This was the 'daily bread' for which they petitioned the Father in the prayer handed down to them from Jesus. 'And day by day, attending the temple together and breaking bread in their homes, they partook of food with glad and generous hearts, praising God and having favour with all the people' (Acts 2:46–47).

After two thousand years the Church's liturgy still conforms to the original format. It begins with the Penitential Rite, the confession of sin before God and one another. The Prodigal Church goes home to its Father. Then the Liturgy of the Word, where the dread silence of sin is broken and loving converse resumes as it always does when the estranged are reconciled. Here, as Vatican II reminds us, through the reading of scripture, 'the Father who is in heaven comes lovingly to meet his children, and talks with them' (*Dei verbum*, §21). Finally, the celebration climaxes at the table of eucharistic sharing. The fatted calf is consumed with hymns of thankful jubilation.

The structure of the experience is sacred because revealed. It is incarnational in that it respects the nature of the human subject seeking contact with God. Each part of the ritual leads into the central truth of the mystery. This is why, for example, Eucharist ought not be received without penance if one is out of harmony with the rest of the Church. And why too one who is reconciled ought not to refrain from receiving. In the first instance it would be akin to the Prodigal Son going straight to the banquet without first approaching his father with apology. In the second, it would be as if that son refused to eat the calf prepared for him after his father's embrace. Worst of all is when Christians stay away from the Eucharist altogether. To those who ask today: what is the point of religious worship, Luke's Gospel replies that it matters to God. He waits, as a father waits, for the children he loves, whom he desires to come home. He wishes to speak with them again heart to heart, to feed their hunger, to make them laugh, to give them joy. He longs to end their alienation from each other, to show compassion, to draw compassion from them, to show them his Son.

Salvation *is* communion. We attain healing through others. In them we find Christ, therefore through them we find God. His tenderness is never imparted except through the instrumentality of fellow human beings. We are, for each other, Christ's hands and feet, his eyes, his ears, his voice: to bless and heal, to approach, to see the needs, to listen to the pain, to console. Compassion is given to be broken and shared. As we have received, so we must impart.

Therefore to cut oneself off from the life of the Church, to stay away from the Eucharist and the sacraments, not to hear the gospel, nor exchange the sign of peace, nor contribute to the communal life of charity, is a sad thing. It impoverishes the spirit of the banquet, dilutes the flow of grace for others as well as for oneself. One is missed when one is not there. It is also sad because to turn down the invitation of him who so humbly invites is to fling his generosity back in his face. Like the elder brother in the parable who refused to come and join in the celebration and the feast. His gentle father reasoned with him, cajoled him, encouraged him with kindliness and warmth; for he had two sons whom he loved and the return of the spendthrift – joyful though that was – did not compensate for the absence of the other. Each was special in his own way. The meal was not complete unless both were there.

That parable ends without a resolution. We do not know if the older lad went in. The evangelist deliberately left it so. For it touches on the enigma of human freedom in every age: to respond, or not to respond to the God whom the parable depicts as waiting constantly for all his beloved sons and longing for their return.

Equally sad for the Church is when those who *do* share

Eucharist together fail to minister compassion to one another. Where grudges are carried into the communion meal, or jealousy, or lack of forgiveness, or a stubborn unwillingness to understand or make allowances. Such attitudes are a counter-witness to the reality expressed by the liturgy. They diminish the credibility of the sacrament as a channel of God's compassion. Therefore they deny the cross. Sometimes it is because the begrudging feel that to forgive is a defeat or a denial of the offence committed. What they forget is that letting-go is not the same as giving in. Jesus did not give in to sin when he reconciled us to the Father. He let it go by taking it upon himself and crucifying it on the tree. And this is what he meant us to do for each other, in him.

Compassion requires that we make ourselves small in the presence of another's weakness. That instead of judging, we recognise our own weakness in theirs, acknowledge fellowship in a common sinfulness that obliges us all to seek mercy. From that position we are then better placed to find Christ, who emptied himself of glory, who lowered himself to make contact with all that is broken, or wretched, or poor, to heal and restore and raise up. There can be no compassion without poverty of spirit nor any gentleness without suffering. We cannot set another person free unless we know what it is to be held captive ourselves. Only those who have honestly faced the frailty of the human condition in themselves and experienced the Father's tenderness towards them, know how to forgive. It was to these that Jesus addressed his message and dedicated his ministry.

In his maiden speech at the synagogue at Nazareth he names the ones he means: the poor, the captives, the blind, the oppressed (Luke 4:18–19). For them he was appointed Messiah and Saviour. 'The Spirit of the Lord is upon me, because he has anointed me to preach good news . . . to proclaim release . . . recovering of sight . . . to set at liberty.' This was the Spirit that descended on him in the river at his baptism; that led him into the wilderness to be tested; that empowered him as he returned to Galilee. It was poured out so that he might make good the ancient promise which he took as the manifesto of his ministry; for as he announced to his listening congregation, 'Today this scripture has been fulfilled in your hearing' (v.18. Cf. Is. 61:1–2a).

True Israelites among them would have recognised the Spirit he spoke of. It was the compassionate Breath of YHWH, alive in the consolation of the prophets and active once again in the Person of Jesus. They could actually hear YHWH's comforting in his voice. He was reciting the most cherished oracle of Deutero-Isaiah, composed five centuries before to encourage the repatriates returning from Exile. Carried on the breath of this Son of encouragement, the text seemed to find not just its fulfilment but its very source in his spirit as he read it back to them now.

To hear again this passage of Isaiah – but in a new context – assuring God's solace to a nation emerging exhausted from a desperate ordeal, seeking to rebuild from the ruins of defeat, was to know that the kingdom they longed for was already in their midst. The endless pain, their energetic prayer had not been in vain. As God had answered them before, so he was answering them again. Not as he answered their fathers when he brought them back to Israel: now he was answering their greater need in bringing them back to himself.

That text on Jesus' lips – sometimes referred to reverentially as Isaiah's Fifth Suffering Servant Song – inaugurates the eschatological kingdom of the Spirit, the final era of salvation ushered in by Jesus' messianic mission. So powerful is the word as it is pronounced that it carries the force of action. It completes itself in being spoken. Jesus is the visible sign of the truth he proclaims, his patient tenderness visible proof of the Spirit's immanence. For all who hear and believe, the ultimate victory guaranteed by the Father is already in place. But only for the poor in spirit who know their need for God, only those in touch with their own insufficiency, who have suffered for want of consolation and mercy. They are the ones who on hearing the speech at Nazareth 'spoke well of him, and wondered at the gracious words which proceeded out of his mouth' (4:22). They were however in the minority for the evangelist – probably conflating two separate accounts of Jesus' visits to his home town – observes that his townsmen rose up angrily against him and tried to throw him over the hill their city was built on.

For the truly poor the discourse in the synagogue was the charter of salvation. It set the agenda for Jesus' ministry in a Gospel that has often been called the Gospel of the Holy Spirit. All the elements of the Spirit's working in Jesus – gentle compassion, generosity, understanding, forgiveness, good humour, witty hyperbole, real humanity – were pledged by that speech in advance. The Spirit himself broke through to them, speaking words which though familiar they had never heard before, never felt the power of until now.

If Luke's Gospel sets the pattern of salvation as it is mirrored in the Act of Worship over which the Paraclete presides, the maiden speech would prefigure the Liturgy of the Word that begins with an Old Testament reading and ends with the Gospel itself. At Nazareth that day the '*anawim YHWH* – the descendants of God's poor and destitute – would have experienced in Jesus' homily the stirrings of spiritual renewal that the penitent feel as the scriptures are read at Mass. They

149

would have known, as all penitents know, that here they are welcome, that their liberation was at hand.

In his words to them was all that was to come: the healings, the teaching to bring new heart, the acceptance of them as they were, the call to show their better selves, and above all the promise of a Calvary that would make that possible.

No longer need the leper fear social alienation. Jesus would take his spiritual leprosy on himself, restoring him to the community of the living; he would change places with him outside the camp at the Calvary where lepers belong. No longer need the discredited fear divine alienation. Like Zacchaeus, men short of moral stature who had to climb trees to see Jesus would find in the lowly Christ a God who climbed a tree himself to make himself seen as Saviour. Nor need the prostitute any longer fear alienation from herself. Women reduced by the personal humiliation of uncleanliness would see Jesus more contaminated yet, an unclean corpse in the unclean bowels of the tomb.

Prostitutes, tax-collectors, lepers, good thieves and bad, prodigal sons and crucifiers: all of them impoverished or captive or blind were to discover in Jesus a depth of humanity, a strength of divinity, that would re-integrate them with themselves, with others, with God. Exposed to his goodness they would come to see their true condition and its roots: sinful because not-integrated; blind because isolated; self-imprisoned because unaccepted; helpless – and therefore deeply cared for by the Father who created them to be free. In the extraordinary freedom of Jesus the man they would recognise the Prototype in whose image they were made, through whom they would be restored, re-created. In his compassionate touch, breath, voice, word they would feel once again what Adam felt when the Lord God shaped him from the dust of the ground and breathed into him the warm and invigorating spirit of life.

This was the Jesus God publically acclaimed as his Beloved Son a second time at the transfiguration. In the Liturgy that Luke's Gospel is, that scene occurs exactly half-way between the speech at Nazareth which begins Christ's ministry, and the crucifixion on Calvary which completes it. It marks a bursting forth of the glory which his gentleness and humility obscured, and which the suffering of the cross would obscure even more from all but the most perceptive.

Throughout the Old Testament the glory of God was seen in his work of deliverance, his salvation. It shone out like a brightness that illuminated the image men had of him. Through the experience of what he did for them and how he did it, they compared his greatness to the radiance of the sun. He brought light out of darkness, life out of death, day out of night, summer out of winter. His brightness magnified his goodness, made it manifest to all creation, bestowed it upon all who turned towards him.

Although this glory was a terrible thing, an awesome force that struck men dumb, inspired holy fear in his faithful and despair in his foes, it was a force of fatherly mercy, deeply tender and affectionate, profoundly compelling. When Moses, for instance, petitioned him after Egypt, 'I pray thee, show me thy glory' (Exod. 33:18), what he saw and heard was not the surging wall of water in which Pharaoh was drowned nor the vulcanic majesty of Sinai exploding, but something more wonderful and lasting. 'The Lord passed before him, and proclaimed, "The Lord, the Lord, a God merciful and gracious, slow to anger, and abounding in steadfast love and faithfulness, keeping love for thousands, forgiving iniquity and transgression and sin"' (Exod. 34:6–7). It was this holiness Moses beheld face to face when he received the Law on the tablets of stone on the mountain. The very skin of his face shone with its reflected light as he descended bearing God's dazzling righteousness as a gift to be shared with his people. It was proof of YHWH's paternal loving-kindness.

Elijah recognised the same glory in the gentle breeze and the still, small voice as he stood at the mouth of his cave on the same holy mountain of Horeb-Sinai. There he experienced unexpected renewal at a time of deep desolation when, dejected and dispirited, he poured out his heart to the Lord.

> And when Elijah heard [the still, small voice], he wrapped his face in his mantle and went out and stood at the entrance of the cave. And behold, there came a voice to him, and said, 'What are you doing here, Elijah?' He said, 'I have been very jealous for the Lord, the God of hosts; for the people of Israel have forsaken thy covenant, thrown down thy altars, and slain thy prophets with the sword; and I, even I only, am left; and they seek my life, to take it away.' (1 Kings 19:13–14)

As with Moses before him on this sacred height, Elijah discovered a humane Deity, gentle with his servant, immensely gentle with his people, re-creative in the face of their failures, salvific when confronted by their wounds. So powerful was YHWH's meekness, so utterly contagious, it impressed itself on the character of his prophets themselves: Elijah, reduced by the apostasy of the nation, lying under the broom tree in the wilderness, accepting his defeat and awaiting his death (1 Kings 19:4–8). And Moses who, despite his gigantic reputation, was described as 'very meek, more than all men that were on the face of the earth' (Num. 12:3).

At the transfiguration it was to the glory of Jesus' meekness that Moses and Elijah bore witness, each flanking him whom the Law and the prophets foretold. St Luke does not omit to tell what these figures were speaking to Jesus about. 'They spoke of his departure (his passing), which he was to accomplish at Jerusalem' (9:31). In other words, his crucifixion; that which was necessary for the Old Testament scriptures to be fulfilled. Necessary too for the new passing, the new Passover, the new departure from sin, for the new Exodus from evil.

As Moses and Elijah had beheld God's glory prefigured in their own day, so now that glory was unveiled in full in Christ crucified. Then they had seen God's humility only from behind as he passed, their faces in their cloaks; now, as St Paul said, that splendour would be looked on directly: 'And we all, with unveiled face, beholding the glory of the Lord, are being changed into his likeness from one degree of glory to another' (2 Cor. 3:18). It was the splendid effulgence of the Father's forgiveness that shone out on the face of the Son, that illuminated his entire humanity, that radiated even from his clothing. 'As Jesus was praying, the appearance of his countenance was altered, and his raiment became dazzling white' (Luke 9:29).

Only a Calvary could demonstrate the sublime majesty of divine mercy. The cross was necessary because it was the truth. This was how far God was prepared to go in loving. Only a Good Friday could complete the kind of promises he had made in the past. By the same token the splendour of the transfiguration was true as well. It brought out the real meaning of the blood and the sweat of the passion. At a glance pain obscures truth. It so draws attention to itself that it blinds the sensitive mind; so scandalises the heart that it immediately alienates those who witness it. They do not see the inner dimensions of suffering, the perfection love must reach to embrace it, the utter transformation that such love effects, the redemptive nature of a God in pain, the absolute victory over sin when that nature is manifested in the flesh and activitated.

This is why Jesus took Peter, James and John with him to the mountain and showed them his glory when he did. It happened immediately after Christ's first prediction of his death. He had just forewarned them of the darkness to come. Now they needed reassurance, as all who encounter the cross do, of the brightness of self-sacrifice too. He had mentioned resurrection to them in the same breath as his suffering. They had not even understood what that meant. They would understand it even less on Good Friday; but later they would recall the glory on the mountain. That vision would sustain their hope through all the Calvaries that lay ahead of them in the Apostolic Church when their message would be ridiculed and rejected.

It was recalled, for example, by the writer of the Second Letter of St Peter, written late in the century when the delay in Christ's Second Coming called into question the Church's affirmation of his power over injustice. To those who suggested that he would never appear, and who thereby implied that his victorious death had been in vain, the writer confidently cited the threefold witness to Jesus' glory at the transfiguration: not just the witness of the Apostles, nor even of the Old Testament scriptures, but of God himself.

For we did not follow cleverly devised myths when we made known to you the power and coming of our Lord Jesus Christ, but we were eyewitnesses of his majesty. For when he received honour and glory from God the Father and the voice was borne to him by the Majestic Glory,

154

'This is my beloved Son, with whom I am well pleased,' we heard this voice borne from heaven, for we were with him on the holy mountain. And we have the prophetic word made more sure. You will do well to pay attention to this as to a lamp shining in a dark place, until the day dawns and the morning star rises in your hearts. (1:16–19)

The power of Christ was not ineffectual. It would establish itself wherever forgiveness overcame hatred, or gentleness conquered violence, or self-sacrifice defeated pride and greed and self-interest. Nor was his coming delayed. It had already begun in the living out of the gospel, in the works of the Spirit, wherever the healing of men's hearts was accomplished in the power and celebration of the Paschal Mystery. The eschatological Coming-in-Power would take place only when the age of the Church had run its course, when the way had been fully prepared for God's final victory by extending Christ's passion to the ends of the earth.

This was the reality the voice at Tabor acknowledged in acknowledging Jesus. Here was a justice greater than Law, a truth more revealing than prophecy. In the gentle nature of Jesus God owned his own nature. 'This is my Son, my Beloved; listen to him!' (Luke 9:35). The very stamp of the Father's identity made visible in the compassionate flesh of the Son. The ineffable glory of divine mercy transfiguring its human embodiment. That which no man before could gaze on without dying, now countenanced on the countenance of Christ that all might live forever!

The heavenly acclamation was from the opening of the First Suffering Servant Song, the one that emphasised the Servant's tender strength, his great patience with the weak. This was the text that would colour Luke's description of the passion, not the Fourth Song which so influenced Matthew and Mark. Here the Servant 'will not cry or lift up his voice in the street', so placid will his coming be. 'A bruised reed he will not break, and a dimly burning wick he will not quench.' His understanding of human nature will spring from his own experience, from among men, not from above them or beyond them or outside the human race. And yet his self-identification with the poor and the weak will not compromise his integrity. 'He will faithfully bring forth justice' for them and for God through his Personal acceptance of poverty and weakness in himself. That which defeats others, he will transform into the means whereby all is transfigured, for 'he will not fail or be discouraged till he has established justice in the earth'. Indeed, God says,

> I have put my Spirit upon him
> (so that) he will bring forth justice to the nations.
> (Therefore) Behold my servant, whom I uphold,
> my chosen, in whom my soul delights.
>
> (Is. 42:1–4: full text)

If at the baptism of Jesus the Father voiced his approval of the cross, at the transfiguration he stood over his promise of resurrection. Though still a future reality for Jesus the man, the glory of the crucifixion assured it. And not only for him but for all whom he embraced. The Voice at the Jordan delighted at the washing of humanity in the Word's solidarity with sinners; at Tabor it rejoiced at the apotheosis of all human being in the Word's solidarity with God. As at the beginning of the Gospel the Voice of Truth gave witness to the Truth embodied in Jesus' life-giving death, so at the centre of the Gospel it revealed the fulness of that Truth: that the inverse side of suffering for love is to become Love. All who would look on the scandal of this self-emptying and recognise in it the out-pouring of grace would in their own turn be transfigured. Accepting the scandal for the sake of the glory as Jesus did, they would indeed not just be like God, but would themselves *become* God in God.

When the Christ of St Luke stretched out his arms on the cross it was not only to embrace a poor and sinful world. He was also raising up his hands to the Father, as to the Source of divine love. It was the gesture of one who prays – the *Orantes*. Beloved Son reaching up to Beloved Father, offering liturgically the triumph of tenderness to the One whose nature is tenderness itself. Filial gentleness returning to gentle Paternity all that was entrusted to him for salvation. Entrusting himself with perfect confidence to the God of compassion. 'Father, into your hands I commend my spirit!' (23:46).

In that gesture prayer reached its perfection, liturgy its perfect form. Turning the sin of his murderers into a priestly act he undermined the very nature of sin. Presenting his entire self in sacrifice he made acceptable the offering of the new Israel, purified by his prayer for pardon and healed by his absolute trust that God would accept so reconciling a gift. Here all was serene and holy abandonment: not the searing kind depicted by Matthew and Mark, but that of Love itself as it handed back into the hands of Love all that Love reclaimed as its own.

The raising of those hands in an evening oblation superseded the outstretched arms of Moses interceding for the Hebrews in battle. Moses' hands grew weary so that they had to be supported by Aaron and Hur (Exod. 17:12). Not so with Jesus. His hands were supported by God himself. And the prayer of Christ superseded the prayer of Elijah whose oration closed the heavens and brought drought on his enemies

(1 Kings 17:1). At Jesus' intercession Paradise was thrown open to good and bad alike, the grace of the Spirit rained down refreshment, heaven blossomed on earth.

Could the God of Elijah, who drew his prophet up to heaven in a chariot of fire, refuse admittance to Jesus and all who were in him? Could the God of Moses, who spoke to his servant as a man speaks to his friend, not answer the Son and all who made his prayer their own? Could the God whom Jesus preached as Father of the poor ignore the poverty of the cross which is the glory of love? Not according to the Gospel of Luke, for here was something greater than Moses, greater than Elijah.

As the dying Christ felt his end approach he began to recite Psalm 30. More than others in the Psalter it is the one that exudes firm hope in God. His oration was cut short at verse 5, the psalmist's commendation of his soul to the Lord. In Luke's re-telling, Jesus substituted the name 'Father' for 'Lord'. Into his Father's hands he surrendered all. It was the last conscious act of a well-Beloved Son, the highest predication of a well-Beloved Father.

Words lovingly uttered, that would never be taken back, now returned to the God who inspired them. He who had given his word to mankind would now keep his word, would honour it, by accepting it in sacrifice from the lips of the crucified Christ. By raising him from the dead, by exalting him in glory, by honouring him with the name which is above all names, God would fulfil the promises of his covenant with the world. The multitude of wounds on the body corporate of mankind would be dressed; tenderest compassion would heal the tenderest of scars; rejuvenated, the children of men would experience once more the gentleness of Fatherly care. Like those whom One lifts as an infant close against his cheek, whom One stoops down to feed, who are led with reins of kindness, with leading-strings of love, they would hear again the Paternal Voice consoling them: 'I will heal their disloyalty, I will love them with all my heart, for my anger has turned from them' (Hos. 11:3–4; 14:5. JB). And like a child who is moved to the depths by the depths of such generosity, men would cry out to God in union with Christ, in the spirit of Calvary – 'O My Beloved Father!'

Excursus:
The Women at Calvary

A CCORDING TO LUKE there were two groups of women at Calvary: the women of Jerusalem, and the women from Galilee. Their presence at the passion is emphasised in the narrative; it draws attention to the absence of Jesus' male disciples. In a Gospel that elevates the gentle strength of mercy, their silent witness is no embellishment by the author; it is an intrinsic part of the symbolism of compassion. Where the men were unable to cope with the pain, the women were unable to dissociate themselves from it. By the very nature of their sex, by their very identity as women, they personified something of the Spirit that led Christ to his sacrifice.

The Daughters of Jerusalem were a group of charitable matrons who provided relief for criminals on the way to their death. They accompanied them to the place of execution to alleviate their suffering with a palliative made of wine mixed with myrrh. They made no distinction between one convict and another; they simply acknowledged human need at its greatest and showed pity. Their great humanity was rewarded when, on one of these excursions, the convict they encountered was Jesus.

Their perception of his cross was neither entirely from

above nor from below, but from within. Had it been from below they would not have followed Jesus. Had it been from above they would not have wept. Jesus even said to them, 'Do not weep for me' (Luke 23:28). He did not weep for himself; the Father did not weep for him; neither must they. It was the Word of God to them from on high descending through the Voice of the Son. It endorsed Luke's insistence on the necessity of suffering, on its liturgical character as a proclamation of redemption. But they would not have understood this yet.

Their compassion for Jesus was simply from within, a natural expression of womanly humanity. In their femininity he recognised a capacity for suffering as vast as his own. And so he added consolingly, 'Daughters of Jerusalem, weep for yourselves and for your children'. Their tears had moved him to an overflow of tenderness more characteristic of their sex than his own. Pity made them vulnerable as it had made him. He suddenly saw what they would have to endure when their city fell to the Romans – for women and children have always been the Christs of history – and he tried to forewarn them. In the scheme of the Gospel their distress for him brings out God's deeper distress for those who bring calamity on themselves, for the lack of repentance in men which incurs the unutterable penalty of its own justice. 'For if they do this when the wood is green', he warned sadly, – (that is, if crucifixion is the fate of the innocent) – 'what will happen when the wood is dry?' – (meaning, what will be the fate of the unrepentant?) (Luke 23:31).

Standing naked before women in the humiliation of his manhood, he revealed the nature of the pity that undergirded his manliness, the divine femininity of a God who grieved more over the estranged than these mothers of Jerusalem did over a Son of their own race.

The women of Galilee who stayed with him to the end, who had accompanied him in his ministry from the beginning, were the prime witnesses of the Paschal Mystery. No detail of the passion escaped them. They observed for future re-telling the words, the gestures, the body language of salvation. Twice their presence is recorded for emphasis. 'And all his acquaintances and the women who had followed him from Galilee . . . saw these things. . . . The women who had come with him from Galilee followed, and saw the tomb, and how his body was laid' (Luke 23:49; 55). They were also the first to find the empty sepulchre on Easter morning, becoming the proto-evangelists, the *apostolae Apostolorum* – the Apostles' apostles. In a society where the testimony of females was inadmissible and so disregarded, their stewardship of the Good News was an embarrassment to the community of disciples. And yet, as Luke's Acts makes plain in its opening chapter, their credentials perfectly fitted the criteria of Apostleship: 'One of the men who have accompanied us during all the time that the Lord Jesus went in and out among us . . . one of these men must become with us a witness to his resurrection' (vv. 21–22) – except that they were not men!

The Third Gospel pointedly overrides the embarrassment of the Apostolic Church by its acknowledgement of the role that women played all along in Jesus' life. Luke names the females among the disciples 'who provided for them out of their means' (8:3) much as he had earlier listed the personal identity of the Twelve (6:13–16). Juxtaposed in this way the parallel lists read like a communal roll-call that implies a complementarity of ministries. Working together as Christ's

company and in Christ's company, men *and* women in Luke
prepare the way for the coming of the kingdom, bring it
about.

The evangelist's forthrightness on this point was no matter
of expediency to boost the Gospel on its wider Gentile
course, no patronising concession to the liberal world of
Greco-Roman culture. It was a matter of Revelation; it was
part of the gospel itself.

When God created man in his own image – according to
the sixth-century Priestly writer's account – it was as male
and female he created them (Gen. 1:27). God, being pure
spirit, is asexual; therefore both the male and the female
reflect something of what the Deity is. The divine image in
mankind is rendered complete only by the sexes-in-union.
This is why dominion over the earth was accorded to the
two as a couple in Eden. Their intercourse would produce
fruitfulness, order and growth. It would perfect the splendour
of the first creation, localising the life-giving unity of the
Creator-God and his Creative-Wisdom.

For the New Testament Christ is that Image incarnate,
the very stamp and impress of YHWH himself. But not as
an unattached male. To be fully visible in his likeness to God
Jesus required his *alter Christus*, his feminine counterpart.
Without it, what was revealed by the incarnation would be
meaningless. Theologically this was supplied by his espousal
of the Church, his completion as God-made-man. Luke's
mentor, St Paul, had already depicted him as the Church's
bridegroom, spouse of her whom he cleansed from every
spot and wrinkle with his blood; head of the Church which
is his body as a husband is head of his wife; the one who
joined himself to humanity that the two might become one
flesh. Henceforth Christ is not to be considered apart from

his Church, any more than a head can be considered apart from a body, or a husband apart from a wife.

An all-male discipleship does not make the symbolism clear. For the nuptial metaphor to work, if the likeness of God is to appear, the influence of the feminine must make itself felt. By their positive interaction with Jesus in his ministry, by their passive communion with him at the cross, the women of Jerusalem and from Galilee did precisely that. In Luke they prefigure the Church as Christ's help-mate in the work of redemption, his 'flesh of my own flesh' for the fruitfulness, order and growth of the new creation.

But that is not all. There is another sense in which the women support and evoke the image of God in Jesus the man. There co-exists in every human being a mixture of the male and the female in different degrees according to gender, the male predominating in the man, the female in the woman. The two were perfectly balanced in Jesus' mature humanity, exquisitely blended – but within the limits of a masculine nature. This is why, for example, in the male-oriented society of his time he was able to offer a leadership that commanded respect, one based on qualities associated with manliness: authority, initiative, integrity, courage, resilience, firmness of purpose. All of which Luke discerned in him and recorded in detail.

At the same time, because his humanity was so keenly attuned to his divine Personhood, the feminine dimension of God in Jesus was clearly in evidence too – in his gentleness, tenderness, pity, understanding and forgiveness. In their purest form these are the marks of maternal love. According to Luke this was the metaphor Jesus used to describe his feelings before his passion.

As he set his face towards Jerusalem and remembered the

prophets who had perished there before him, he gave way to his compassion for the city that consistently rejected God's messengers.

> O Jerusalem, Jerusalem, killing the prophets and stoning those who are sent to you! How often would I have gathered your children together *as a hen gathers her brood under her wings*, and you would not! (13:34)

He could not have chosen a more intimate symbol of grieving affection. The mother-hen image touches the most primeval instinct in man. To cast himself in such a role was to reach into the very womb of his own femininity to express the anguish that consumed him.

Again, upon reaching the Mount of Olives that overlooked the city, he broke down and cried unashamedly.

> And when he drew near and saw the city he wept over it, saying, 'Would that even today you knew the things that make for peace!. . . . For the days shall come upon you, when your enemies . . . will dash you to the ground, you and your children within you, and they will not leave one stone upon another in you.' (19:41–44)

Only a supremely sensitive person could have spoken and acted thus. When the God in Christ gazed on the fate of his children – a sight too terrible even for God to watch – nothing less than maternal language could depict his pain. To the Daughters of Jerusalem he would later proclaim, 'Blessed are the barren, and the wombs that never bore, and the breasts that never gave suck!' (Luke 23:29). The suffering endured for the fruit of one's womb is the bitterest there is; it is a cross too heavy to bear. Jesus, idealised as a woman weeping for her infants, a Rachel inconsolable, revealed at that moment in the

God of the Hebrews a Fatherhood so tender that it must henceforth be re-imaged as *also* a divine Motherhood.

The idea was not alien to the Old Testament (though it is rare), but Jesus confirmed it as a truth by his appearance in the flesh. The Exodus experience, for example, was likened to an eagle supporting her chicks on their first flight. Addressing the liberated Israelites at Sinai the Lord reminds them of their dependence at that time: 'You have seen what I did to the Egyptians, and how I bore you on eagles' wings and brought you to myself' (Exod. 19:4). In the Song of Moses – a very ancient liturgical text – the concept is enshrined in elaborate, poetic terms:

> Like an eagle that stirs up its nest,
> that flutters over its young,
> spreading out its wings, catching them,
> bearing them on its pinions,
> the Lord alone did lead him.
>
> (Deut. 32:11–12)

Even more specific was Deutero-Isaiah, the consoler *par excellence* of Israel who did not shrink from giving the divine mother-imagery its full scope:

> Can a woman forget her sucking child [says the Lord],
> that she should have no compassion on the son of her
>   womb?
> Even these may forget,
> yet I will not forget you (49:15); and:

> Thus says the Lord [about Israel and Jerusalem]:
> 'Behold, I will extend prosperity to her like a river,
> and the wealth of the nations like an overflowing stream;

and you shall suck, you shall be carried upon her hip,
and dandled upon her knees.
As one whom his mother comforts,
so I will comfort you;
you shall be comforted in Jerusalem.'

(Is. 66:12–13)

Though the God of Israel was a male Deity, masculine in
his deliverance, patriarchal in his judgement, aggressive in his
anger, severe in his chastisements, yet he was all love and was
therefore Mother as well as Father to his people. Like the
psalmist, when they needed encouragement and comfort as
children often do, they discovered the depth of his maternal
peace.

Truly [says Israel] I have set my soul
in silence and peace.
As a child has rest in its mother's arms,
even so my soul.

O Israel, hope in the Lord
both now and forever.

(Ps. 130/131)

In the meekness of Jesus' flesh, in his attitude to the repentant,
in his concern for the unrepentant, what had previously been
sensed of God's Motherhood was proved true. In the body of
Christ, in his ministry, in his death, all the feminine metaphors
in fact are mixed – wife, woman, mother – to accommodate
the mystery which the incarnation enfolds. And as the metaphor thus rounds to its fulness in him, so it becomes fully
salvific, for ultimately it is not about gender, but grace. The
strong, understanding love of God in Christ, being all things

167

to all men, encapsulates the types of feminine love which are its own reflection – that of wives for husbands, mothers for children, sisters for brothers – even as it infiltrates those types, making them grace-filled and salvific too.

Therefore women are sacraments of the divine femininity. As sisters and wives and mothers they locate the sensitivity of Christ who is himself the Sacrament of God. They embody his gentleness, universalise it, make it visible in the kingdom of God on earth. Women are gentle by nature, for while gentleness is not absent in men it is more truly instinct in the female personality. Grace sanctifies that instinct and perfects it. This is why Luke mentions the women so often, more so than the other synoptics, and makes them the sole witnesses in faith to Christ's self-sacrificing death.

Throughout the whole of the ministry Luke used their association with Jesus to show forth Christ's own tender nature. Each contact between them is a little epiphany of the incarnation. Their very presence evokes from him his greatest kindnesses: to the poor widow of Nain whose son he raised from the dead; to the timid, courageous woman with the issue of blood for whom he searched in the crowd until he found and blessed her for her faith; or the twelve-year-old daughter of Jairus whom he restored to life and health for sheer pity's sake. It is Luke alone who records these encounters and points out the effect they had on the Saviour.

Given Luke's purpose, it is almost inevitable that we should find the women all present at Calvary. As they drew forth the grace of the Saviour's humanity in life, so now they accept the fulness of his self-giving for them in death. Standing alone without the men, supporting him by their silent, fragile strength, they testify to the same indomitable spirit in the One crucified. Reflected in their powerful helplessness is the truth embedded in the cross: that God's weakness is stronger than men's strength, as his foolishness is wiser than men's wisdom.

These women represent, they are the poor in spirit, without status, undistinguished, whose help is in God alone. Christ died for such as these. For them he had particular affection. They reminded men of what all must become if they want to value the gospel and share in the fruits of redemption. Upon them was poured a full share of the Holy Spirit which would flood the world through Christ's Church.

This is why Luke ends his Gospel with the end of the historical Jesus and continues the story of salvation in the Book of Acts with the Christian Community at Pentecost. That Community marks the new era of the Spirit when all that Jesus accomplished locally will be universalised. The women of Calvary are the link between the two phases of the story. They appear again in the upper room in Jerusalem with the men, about one hundred and twenty in all (Acts 1:14–15), all of them devoted to prayer and later to the apostolic deposit of faith, the common life of sharing, and to the liturgy of the breaking of bread (Acts 2:42). Now the image of God is complete. Revealed in Christ, extended through the Spirit, manifested in the co-operative lives of men and women in unity, the authority of God and the healing of God are released into the world to the ends of the earth and the consummation of the ages. Not just God's discipline but also his mercy, not just his judgement but his forgiveness too, his love as well as his truth.

In the blending of the male and the female the mystery of the cross will espouse the world, give birth to many offspring, humanise the race and divinise the citizens of the kingdom.

In many beloved sons and daughters, the Beloved Son will henceforth cry out forever with confident self-surrender even in the glory of pain, 'O God, my Beloved Father! O my Beloved Mother! Into your hands I commend my spirit!'

CHAPTER FOUR

'O My Beloved Son!'

The Johannine Passion Tradition

FROM THE START, John's Gospel is a sublime portrayal of the glory of Jesus and his Father. That glory explodes at the end with apocalyptic brilliance at Jesus' death, for the cross in John is the nucleus of divine glory. Here God reigns triumphantly from a tree.

Written late in the first century, the Johannine Passion leaves far behind the gruesome details of Mark-Matthew, goes beyond the tenderness of Luke's gentle Saviour, and takes us to the heart of awesome Majesty. It exposes us unprotected to the light which is the life of men, the eternal life that enlightens all who gaze at it directly. It is a light that blinds the seer to his former existence, bedazzling him with bright insight into grace and truth.

Here we have the mature conclusion to a good half-century of spiritual reflection on the mystery of Calvary. It is set against a high christology that begins with Jesus' divine pre-existence as God's equal and focuses on his Godly condescension as the Word made flesh. Unlike the synoptics who approach the same reality from the other way round, starting with Jesus' lowly birth at Bethlehem or his humble baptism in the Jordan and concluding with his glorification after death.

What we witness therefore when we reach the Johannine

crucifixion is the unfleshed glory of the eternally begotten Son as he truly is, manifestly arrayed in splendid self-possession, enthroned in kingly command of his universe. John marks the culmination of a process that first considered God's presence in pain, then came to accept the necessity of pain, and finally envisioned pain's beauty. Putting all the traditions together we see the complete Calvary – a progressive, ascending view of the cross that complements John's descending christology. In that cyclic movement salvation turns full circle. The downward plunge (the incarnation), and the upward thrust (the exaltation of the cross), complete the swift, sure act of deliverance that, even from of old, the psalmist knew was characteristic of God:

> From on high he reached down and seized me;
> he drew me forth from the mighty waters.
> He snatched me from my powerful foe,
> from my enemies whose strength I could not match.
>
> (Ps. 17/18)

This is why the Christ of St John is so poised in his passion, so completely in control of the storm that breaks over him. The work he does is the Father's work, full of the kingdom, the power and the glory and therefore sure to succeed. It is the week of the new creation. Once again the Master-workman presides over chaos, confidently preoccupied with his well-ordered plans. As in the primeval myth (to which the Fourth Gospel, like Psalm 17, alludes), divine Wisdom is purposefully repairing, perfecting the *urstuff* of life.

Jesus' composure is clear from John's style and tone. It stands in contrast to the agitated confusion that heaves and swells around him. His speech is eminently balanced and serene, not wild and fanatical like that of Pilate, the high priests and the crowd. His demeanour never loses its dignity. He rises above all that happens to him by entering freely into it.

To emphasise the effect the evangelist splices his source material with editorial sureness, choosing or rejecting to suit his theological purpose. He deliberately omits the agony in the garden for example. In its place is the magnificent farewell discourse which ends with the self-assured Priestly Prayer of John 17.

Again, when the soldiers and officers arrive to arrest him, Jesus is seen to go forward to face them. He knows 'all that is to befall him' (18:4). It is he who initiates the contest with darkness ('Whom do you seek?'), identifying himself with the sacred formula that enshrines the holy Name of YHWH, 'I am he' (v. 5). So dynamic is this word, his oppressors draw back and fall to the ground. An unseen force holds them at bay. They are powerless in his presence until he permits them to take him. Later he will treat Pilate's threats with the same heavenly disdain.

> 'Do you not know [contends the governor] that I have power to release you, and power to crucify you?' Jesus answered him, 'You would have no power over me unless it had been given you from above.' (19: 10–11)

In himself Jesus is beyond their reach, as he is beyond the reach of evil and sin. The source of his perfect freedom is his innocence and truth. There is nothing hidden about him, nothing sinister or covert. 'I have spoken openly to the world', he tells Annas the high priest; 'I have always taught in the synagogues and in the temple, where all Jews come together, I have said nothing secretly' (18:20). And yet he is absolute mystery. 'Where do you come from?' Pilate demands with rising apprehension (19:8–9). Jesus' simplicity confounds governor and high priest alike. When an officer strikes him for his answer to Annas, Jesus replies, 'If I have spoken wrongly, bear witness to the wrong; but if I have spoken rightly, why do you strike me?' (18: 22–23). The aggressor is left with nothing to say, and Annas shuffles him off to Caiaphas.

'I find no crime in him', Pilate is to admit later to the crowds (18:38) – a vindication the evangelist carefully records. His words are repeated twice after the scourging when Jesus is presented wearing the crown of thorns and the purple robe. 'Pilate went out again, and said to them, "Behold, I am bringing him out to you, that you may know that I find no crime in him". . . . Pilate said to them, "Take him yourselves and crucify him, for I find no crime in him" ' (19:4, 6). His tone is desperate now, his authority immobilised, his free-will stiffled by the malign will of the mob.

Proportionately as the governor's control of the situation collapses, Jesus' mastery over it rises. 'So you are a king?' Pilate challenges, acknowledging the impact of his calm and candid presence. Jesus cannot deny it. 'You say that I am a king. For this I was born, and for this I have come into the world, to bear witness to the truth. Every one who is of the truth hears my voice' (18:37). Truth was his greatest defence, his kingdom, his impregnable fortress, his assurance of victory. They might dispose of his body as they pleased, his Self they could never defeat for this Self was 'the way, the truth and the life' (John 14:6). But Pilate, who would not recognise the Truth if it stood enfleshed before him, 'said to him, "What is truth?" ' (18:38).

In the Johannine writings truth – *aletheia* – means much more than the facts of a matter, more even than honesty or intellectual accuracy. It means a way of life that is enlightened.

It means freedom to do what is right regardless of difficulties or consequences. Since only God can give this freedom, this enlightenment, truth is ultimately knowledge of God. In Christ that knowledge is given as a relationship because God is in Christ, offering intimacy with himself through the incarnation. As Jesus explained to those who listened, 'I am the way, the truth and the life; no one comes to the Father, but by me. If you had known me, you would have known my Father also; henceforth you know him and have seen him. . . . He who has seen me has seen the Father' (John 14:6–7; 9).

In his commentary on this, Thomas Aquinas demonstrates how the three epithets of Jesus' self-description flow in and out of one another with the same harmony of purpose that unites Christ's divine and human natures.

> Christ himself is the way . . . since through him we have access to the Father. Now, because this way is not at a distance from its terminating point but rather joined with it, he adds, 'the truth and the life', and so he is at once the way and its termination. In his humanity he is the way, in his divinity the termination. So, as man he says, 'I am the way', and as God he adds, 'the truth and the life', two words that well describe the termination of that way.
>
> (*Commentary on St John's Gospel*, Chapter 14, Reading 2)

Truth therefore not only guarantees Jesus' integrity as Son of Man in the trumped-up case against him. It also guarantees the outcome of his struggle as Son of God with the powers of darkness. The glory of truth – God's utter holiness – will pierce the cosmic night of sin through his self-sacrifice. The endurance of truth – too great for any physical nature to sustain – will break open his manhood, the universal upward way to God. And because of truth's fidelity to itself unto death, his death will unseal the primordial source of life for all who, with him, bear witness to the truth. The eclipse of the man will make visible the corona of the Godhead; the obscuring of the Son will intensify the radiance of the Father. Never again will divine love be kept at a distance by the tilt of creation away from its God, a result of the impact of falsehood and deceit.

Christ reigns in the St John Passion because he knows the Father. This is the moment when truth, life and love will be firmly established. For John, God *is* love (1 John 4:8, 16), and God is *life* (John 11:25), and God *is truth* (John 1:14). The crucifixion establishes God on earth. It undresses his actual nature, his whole being, raising it up for all to see; so that seeing, all 'may believe that Jesus is the Son of God, and that believing you may have life in his name', as the first conclusion to the Fourth Gospel puts it (20:31).

Because Jesus is one with the Father, he is fully competent to accomplish his task alone. In John there is no Simon of Cyrene. He is not needed. 'So . . . Jesus went out, *bearing his own cross*' (John 19:17). It was the instrument of his eternal sovereignty. It defined the nature of his kingship as 'not of this world' (John 18:36), just as the crown of thorns defined his lordship as one of love through suffering, and the robe of mockery defined his power as infinite patience, and the fragile reed his authority as one of humble service.

Even the scroll that Pilate the pagan displayed above the cross proclaims the truth of Christ's identity. It stands at the crossroads of the world written in Hebrew, Latin and Greek for the world to read. The Jews contest the scroll. It ought not affirm Jesus as King. It should be changed to read that this man claimed to be King of the Jews. But Pilate does not listen to them. 'What I have written', he answered, 'I have written' (John 19:22). In other words truth has been expressed and cannot be unexpressed. The evangelist seizes on the irony of the event. A Roman has stumbled on a truth he does not know the half of, has announced it to the Chosen People and to the nations. His official identification of the Messiah, irretractible because an imperial decree, pronounces theological reality: the Word has become flesh and cannot be revoked. This Word hangs nailed like the scroll above it, articulated, inscribed in the crucified flesh of the Nazarene forever. What *God* has written, he has written, and like an imperial decree it can never be altered.

So irrepressible is the truth in John's Gospel that it is constantly breaking out, being stumbled upon, despite the effort to bury it. As in Gerard Manley Hopkins' poem, all 'is charged with the grandeur of God./ It will flame out, like shining from shook foil' ('God's Grandeur'). No less than Caiaphas catches its glory as he plots Jesus' destruction. Fearing the threat to Judaism that Jesus posed,

> Caiaphas, who was high priest that year, said to [the council], 'You know nothing at all; you do not understand that it is expedient for you that one man should die for the people, and that the whole nation should not perish'. He did not say this of his own accord, but being high priest that year he prophesied that Jesus should die for the nation, and not for the nation only, but to gather into one the children of God who are scattered abroad.
>
> (John 11:49–52)

High priests prophesy it, Romans inscribe it, Christians proclaim it: Jesus of Nazareth is King of the Jews and therefore Lord of the universe. The good news that John tells will not be subverted. Calvary is the key to truth and life. The more it is evaded, denied or mocked, the more it is asserted, verified and established. Unshiftable as fact, truthful as irony, and fear-inspiring, God hangs on the cross in the Fourth Gospel, confounding disbelief by his total dominion over all that is not God. Whether men accept what they see or not, chaos has been innocently over-ruled, utterly broken on its own strength, mortified in the sight of all.

The triumph in the Johannine account is near-apocalyptic. It is hidden in the symbolism of surface details but revealed to the vision of paschal faith, open to the believing mind that seeks the truth. As the Book of Revelation puts it, 'This calls for wisdom' (13:18) – a quality the Fourth evangelist requires of his reader too and presupposes as he arranges his final text.

The date and time of Christ's epiphany as King, for example, are carefully emphasised. 'Now it was the day of Preparation of the Passover; it was about the sixth hour. Pilate said to the Jews, "Here is your King!" ' (John 19:14). Twelve o'clock noon on Preparation day: the time when the lambs were slaughtered for the renewal of the Passover. The Book of Exodus had laid down precise prescriptions for the way this was to be done. 'Your lamb shall be without blemish, a male . . . and you shall not break a bone of it' (12:5; 46). Jesus is the Lamb without blemish. John the Baptist hailed him 'The Lamb of God' (John 1:38) at his appearance by the river Jordan. At his exit on Golgotha his bones remained unbroken according to the precept. Though the legs of the criminals beside him were fractured by the soldier to hasten death, Jesus' limbs were left unscathed. He was already dead and so the Roman lanced his side with a spear instead.

Unblemished, unbroken, intact though sacrificed, the crucified Jesus – like the seamless robe which they did not tear – remains integral. There is no rupture in his form as God and man. Later in the inspired sighting of heaven the same Lamb will appear again – scarred, though glorified and whole.

> And between the throne and the four living creatures and among the elders, I saw a Lamb standing, as though it had been slain . . . and heard the voice of many angels, 'Worthy is the Lamb who was slain, to receive power and wealth and wisdom and might and honour and glory and blessing'.
> (Rev. 5:6; 12–13)

Even if this text is not by the same hand that wrote the Fourth Gospel, it shares a common Johannine tradition, borrows similar literary motifs such as the Lamb and life and truth. And it confirms the eschatological victory of the Immolation which John describes in exalted terms. This lamb is not just the ravaged victim of the synoptic tradition taken from the Suffering Servant Songs. He is rather the Apocalyptic Lamb triumphant, the Lion of Judah rampant (Rev. 5:5), the heraldic seal of God's majestic jubilee.

This explains why John purposely omits the three hours' suspension from the cross-beam which the synoptics assert. Why too he omits the taunting of the chief priests, the scribes and the passers-by, which Matthew, Mark and Luke all use to heighten the pathos and the pain. Nor does John mention the wailing women. These details must not be allowed to distract from the gracious splendour of the King's Coronation. And though he records the words, 'I thirst' (19:28), he presents them as a fulfilment, not a defeat. This is a Coronation speech. The King thirsts for loyalty and for faith, not for water, as he did when he met the Samaritan woman at the well.

> Jesus answered her, 'If you knew the gift of God, and who it is that is saying to you, "Give me a drink", you would

179

have asked him, and he would have given you living water'. . . . The woman said to him, 'I know that Messiah is coming (he who is called Christ); when he comes, he will show us all things.' Jesus said to her, 'I who speak to you am he.' (John 4:10; 25–26)

For John, Jesus radically matches and surpasses the messianic expectations of the Jews, and the world's religious longing. The Fourth Gospel abounds in a plethora of titles prefixed with the sacred 'I am' which show him to be the end, the sum of all human need. He is not only the Messiah, the One Who Is To Come; he is the New Moses, the new Passover, the true Lamb; he is the Way, the Truth and the Life, the Resurrection and the Life, the Light of the World, the Vine, the Living Bread; he is the Door to the Sheepfold, the Good Shepherd, the Word made flesh, the King of the Jews. In him all God's promises are faithfully delivered, all the ancient types of man's desiring rendered suddenly comprehensible, and justified.

Five times throughout the Passion Narrative John states that scripture was being fulfilled (18:9, 32; 19:24, 28, 36–37). The Father was keeping his oath. The Son was carrying it out to the letter. In the fulness of the time, at the precise moment planned, a great cosmic movement of grace was altering the universe.

Even now the Lamb is opening the seven seals. The Lamb is standing on Mount Zion with his hundred and forty-four thousand. Like a scroll rolled up, the sky is vanishing; mountains and islands are being dislocated, removed. The kings of the earth are hiding in terror. The beast and its image, false prophet and dragon, first-death and ancient serpent are being cast into the lake of fire, into the bottomless pit. All things are being made new.

The Gospel may not use the language of the Apocalypse but it shares an identical theological vision. The final act of human history has begun, the drama of salvation is nearing its climax. Christ is the protagonist. God himself is the Actor and the Action. Swiftly and surely he is moving to claim the denouement as his own.

One last thing remains. As in the Book of Revelation provision is made for the Elect – personified in the woman clothed with the sun – before the final catastrophe, so also at Calvary. Jesus must make arrangements for the Church, symbolised by his Mother, before his ultimate conflict with the enemy. Now, having set all things in proper order and fulfilled all that was required, having put all things under his feet, he serenely bows his head and gives up his spirit (19:30). Not 'breathed his last' as in Luke, not 'with a loud voice' as in Matthew, nor uttering 'a loud cry' as in Mark. In John, the anguish of his demise is not even mentioned. The text is so euphemistic, one hardly notices a death at all. It is more a consummation – the word in fact that John uses. 'Consummatum est.' It is a Royal Edict. The kingdom has been inaugurated. Mortality, the last of his enemies, has been quietly destroyed.

Therefore this 'Consummatum est' is not an end but a beginning. Although it belongs to the Finale, what is finalised is the reclamation of all things by God and his Word. It signals the emergence of the new creation, the new heaven, the new earth. Its finality suggests the work's perfection. It echoes God's approval in Genesis when, surveying his original crafts-manship on the sixth day, he expressed his complete satisfaction. 'And God saw everything he had made, and behold, it was very good' (1:31). Now he could lie down in peace and take his rest. As in that account the Creator's seventh-day repose confirmed the intrinsic goodness of his labour unto the end of time, so Christ's sabbath sleep in the tomb would confirm its perfection unto eternity.

While the synoptics do not exclude the notion of a new world order emanating from the Paschal Mystery, they tend to see the coming of the kingdom as belonging to the end of history. The Fourth Gospel however envisages an immanent eschatology, an already-begun retrojection of God's future triumph back into the present. Hence the strong Apocalyptic treatment of the Calvary event. But if in present endings are future beginnings, in this present beginning is also an end, a completion of what God did at the dawn of existence. Past Genesis is brought to immediate fulfilment in the *kairos* of the St John Passion. The idea is built into the very structure of the Gospel, in its initial chapters as well as its Calvary conclusion.

John's Prologue, for example, takes the opening phrase of the Creation account – 'In the beginning' – to introduce the Good News of Christ as the new Genesis. Like the Old Testament writer the evangelist focuses on the impressive power and authority of the divine Word. Once uttered it summons all things to existence. Nine times the ancient author noted the fact that 'God said, "Let there be" . . . and there was'. In the Gospel John identifies that Word as Jesus himself. He was 'with God' from before anything came to be; it was through him that 'all things were made', and without him 'was not anything made that was made' (1:1–3).

Now the same Word is powerfully at work again, re-creating and revealing as God decrees, achieving the divine intention as soon as it is spoken. Not this time summoning non-being to existence but calling the dead to life.

> Truly, truly, I say to you, the hour is coming, and now is,
> when the dead will hear the voice of the Son of God, and
> those who hear will live . . . when all who are in the tombs
> will hear his voice and come forth. (John 5:25, 28)

What the Voice of the Father pronounces over the face of
the deep is not some command or set of instructions, but the
exalted name of his Beloved Son. So effective is this speech
that the Word makes its Personal appearance, proclaiming in
turn the eternally Beloved Fatherhood. The eschaton has
begun. For before now 'no one [had] ever seen God; [but] the
only Son, who is in the bosom of the Father, he has made him
known' (John 1:18).

Overheard from the depths of man's chaos, the great
Affirmation of God from God quickens the old creation to
grace. Voice and Word together, in one undivided action, calls
the children of Adam to immortality. 'Truly, truly, I say to you,
he who hears my word and believes him who sent me, *has*
eternal life' (John 5:24). The evangelist preserves the present
tense in Jesus' teaching. The moment of God's glory is now.

It was on the sixth day of creation that Adam received
the breath of life (reading the conflated Priestly and Jahwist
accounts as one narrative). 'God said, "Let us make man in our
own image, after our own likeness" . . . then the Lord God
formed man of dust from the ground, and breathed into his
nostrils the breath of life' (Gen. 1:26; 2:7). It was also on the
sixth day of the week that Jesus bowed his head and gave forth
his spirit. It fell directly on those below him, standing at the
foot of the cross. God was in-spiring his creature a second
time; not just exhaling as before, but expiring, giving himself
out to his last breath. Once again the Breath-taking love of
Father for Son and of Son for his Father was hovering over the

dark abyss, sweeping down across the formless void of sinful humanity bringing light and life, proceeding from the heart of the Triune God as the loving inclusiveness that gathers into one all things outside himself. Thus Jesus crucified, God from God, completes the work of re-creation.

At the same time he is also man from man, himself a second Adam. When 'the first man . . . became a living being' – to quote St Paul – he passed death on to his children. But by accepting death 'the last Adam became a life-giving spirit' (1 Cor. 15:45). What Paul theologises on, the Fourth Gospel demonstrates. Bereft of his breath, Christ's corpse leaves behind a family that will carry his Spirit to the end of time. In Johannine circles the crucifixion was such a consummate act, it encompassed the mystery of Pentecost as well. The life of Christ's Spirit is Life to the full (John 10:10). In that Spirit men will cry out 'Abba! Father!' (Rom. 8:15) for this reason: that now the natural sons of Adam are become the adopted sons of God; what proves it so is their capacity to 'suffer with [Christ] in order [to] . . . be glorified with him' (Rom. 8:17). Thus death, which in Adam robbed his offspring of life, becomes in Christ their means to its fulness in glory.

The new order of things initiated by the cross has turned the old one inside out. It is now the right way round. Suffering and sonship are no longer conjoined by the distortion of sin, as in exiled Adam after Eden. They are now conjoined by the sanctity of love, restored in Jesus after Calvary. The Johannine perception of the cross therefore as majesty and might – in itself an extraordinary perception – makes sense against the startling paradox of divine wisdom: Adam defeated is Adam restored, the second fall of Man uplifts man from his first.

Jesus is the new Adam in another sense too. From his consummate death emerges the mystical Eve in a manner comparable to that of the first woman, who was taken physically from the body of the first man. She too will be called 'mother of all the living' (Gen. 3:20), for as the Church she will give spiritual birth to those conceived from the seed of faith. After Jesus has yielded up his spirit, 'one of the soldiers pierced his side with a spear, and at once there came out blood and water' (John 19:34). The phenomenon parallels the story in Genesis 2:

> The Lord God caused a deep sleep to fall upon the man, and while he slept took one of his ribs and closed up its place with flesh; and the rib which the Lord God had taken from the man he made into a woman and brought her to the man. Then the man said, 'This at last is bone of my bones and flesh of my flesh; she shall be called Woman because she was taken out of Man'. (vv. 22–23)

John is the only one of the four to mention the lancing at Calvary. Moreover, he draws the reader's particular attention to it. 'He who saw it has borne witness – his testimony is true, and he knows that he tells the truth – that you also may believe' (19:35). Unique to the Fourth Gospel and stressed, it is a matter of considerable importance to the writer and the Christian community he represents. It indicates their sense of the ecclesiality of Jesus' triumph, channelled through the sacramental life of his bride.

The water and blood signify baptism and the Eucharist, the mysteries of initiation by which believers are incorporated into Jesus' body and nourished in their new-found faith. The Early Fathers recognised the implicit meaning of the sign immediately in their exegesis of the text. The fourth-century Patriarch of Constantinople, St John Chrysostom, for example, highlighted its significance in his instruction of those preparing for baptism.

> 'There came from his side water and blood'. . . . It is from these two that the holy Church has been born 'by the washing of regeneration and the renewal of the Holy Spirit', by baptism and the mysteries. Now the symbols of baptism and the mysteries came from his side. It was from his side, then, that Christ formed the Church, as from the side of Adam he formed Eve.
>
> That is why in his first account of the first man Moses has the words, 'bone of my bone and flesh of my flesh', giving us a hint here of the Master's side. For as at that time God took a rib from Adam's side and formed woman, so Christ gave us blood and water from his side and formed the Church. Just as then he took the rib while Adam was in a deep sleep, so now he gave the blood and water after his death.
>
> Have you seen how Christ united his bride to himself?
>
> (*To Catechumens*, chapter 3)

Flowing from the heart of Christ into the hearts of men this twin stream of grace brings the Church into being and supports it in every place where it springs up like growing cells around the Mediterranean. In its wake it leaves signs of life in abundance in the otherwise stagnant pool of the world.

The evangelist must have been thinking of the stream in Ezekiel that came from under the temple threshold and flowed eastward; because the same passage comes up again in the Apocalypse where the Johannine Lamb gathers his heavenly Church along the crystal-bright river of life in the new Jerusalem.

The water flowed from under the right side of the Temple, south of the altar. . . . It was now a river which I could not cross; the stream had swollen and was now deep water. . . . [The angel said to me], 'This water flows east down to the Arabah and to the sea; and flowing into the sea it makes its waters wholesome. Wherever the river flows, all living ceatures teeming in it will live . . . for wherever the water goes it brings health, and life teems wherever the river flows. . . . Along the river on either bank will grow every kind of fruit tree with leaves that never wither and fruit that never fails; they will bear new fruit every month, because this water comes from the sanctuary. And their fruit will be good to eat and the leaves medicinal.'

(Ezek. 47:1–12. JB; cf. Apoc. 22:1–2)

The pierced corpse of Christ stands half-way between the Old Testament prophecy that anticipated his cross, and the Apocalyptic promise that awaits those who believe in it. Centred with Christ between these points of salvation history, and centred on him, the Church of the sacraments holds in fruitful tension the saving grace already achieved, and the hope of glory yet to be revealed.

For a community that regarded everything about Jesus as significant, as the Gospel shows (John 2:11, 18, 23; 4:48, 54), and that saw all he did and said as signs to be reflected upon and interpreted in Spirit, the sacraments were the *signs par excellence* of his presence and activity among them. Their discernment of this proved Christ's prediction true: 'The Counsellor, the Holy Spirit, whom the Father will send in my name, he will teach you all things, and bring to your remembrance all that I have said to you' (John 14:26). These signs confirmed them in their faith. Here Jesus himself was

187

acting. Through their sacred rites he was perpetuating his cross, extending its influence, enlarging their belief in his victory. Even before their (relatively) long oral tradition had distilled the story of the piercing to its final form in the (comparatively) late written Gospel, its liturgical importance in their ecclesial life was clearly and firmly established.

> This is he who came by water and blood, Jesus Christ, not with the water only but with the water and the blood. And the Spirit is the witness, because the Spirit is the truth. There are three witnesses, the Spirit, the water, and the blood; and these three agree. (1 John 5:6–8)

If penned before the Gospel, as many scholars believe, John's First Letter already implies a perspective on Calvary that borders on the mystical. A later redactor (whose marginal gloss is not canonical) would even try to specify the three witnesses as 'the Father, the Word and the Holy Ghost', a Trinitarian formula which belongs rather to the fourth century (when it first appeared in the Vulgate) and would have been unfamiliar to the original inspired author. But the redactor's sense of the fulness of the text in terms of the divine completeness of Christ's sacrifice was legitimate. The community of the Beloved Disciple to whom the Letter was addressed had long since grasped the fulness and the glory of the cross precisely by dint of their existence as Church and their experience of grace through the re-enactment of the signs.

What that experience communicated, what their existence as a faith-communion conveyed, was a deeply held conviction that Christ's life – the life of the Spirit – lives in the life of the Church; that where the signs are preserved in the dynamic practice of faith the river continues to flow. There Christ goes on expending his Spirit to the last gasp, goes on emptying his body of its currents of energy as a life-giving force for his spouse. A similar process of theological reflection has re-vitalised the Church of our own time. At Vatican II the Christian community, like that of the first century, returned to its source, to Calvary, and with that unique sense of the intimacy that bonds the crucified Christ to his faithful, re-considered its own origins and measured again the depth of the stream from which it takes its life. Hence the jubilant acclamation of the first document to emerge from the Coun-cil's contemplation of sacramental liturgy:

> It is the liturgy through which, especially in the divine sacrifice of the Eucharist, 'the work of our redemption is accomplished,' and it is through the liturgy, especially, that the faithful are enabled to express in their lives and manifest to others the mystery of Christ and the real nature of the true Church. . . . For it was from the side of Christ as he slept the sleep of death upon the cross that there came forth 'the wondrous sacrament of the whole Church'. (*Sacrosanctum concilium*, §§2, 5, quoting the Roman Missal for Paschaltide)

Then, as now, the swollen river from the Temple of Christ's body is a credible sign of the power of his cross. That is why John bore witness to it: 'that you also may believe'. The Church is the place where that belief is located. So the Church itself becomes a credible sign of the mystery that is Calvary because it is a communion under Christ crucified, and with him and through him and in him. 'What we have seen and heard we proclaim also to you, so that you have fellowship with us; and our fellowship is with the Father and with his Son Jesus Christ. And we are writing this that our joy (and yours) may be complete' (1 John 1:3–4).

189

Because faith and fellowship are one there can be no regeneration apart from the Church. If Christ is the new Adam, the new Eve is his help-mate. She must share with him the responsibilities and consequences of their marital union. The stream of life that unites them signifies that she is no widow. She and her husband are still together, and though he is not seen by outsiders, her fruitfulness is proof that he is living with her. Teeming life continues to emerge from the baptismal womb of the laver of rebirth. Wholesome food, nourishing and medicinal, continues to be provided twelve times a year (that is, every day) in the breaking of Bread and the cup of salvation. To seek life from him away from her would be like coming between a man and his wife, like breaking up a marriage. No husband can love two wives: it is the nature of love to be monogamous, and Christ is no adulterer. Which is why the Church is one in itself. It is because of him whose love knows no division, and whose love has been given to her as a man gives who loves his wife as his own undivided body.

Because the Christ of John 19 is so sublime, his glory so defined, he not only images the Father in the re-creation of man; he not only fulfils the type which Adam prefigured at the formation of Eve; he also embodies the Motherhood of which Eve is the symbol and of which he, with the Father and the Holy Spirit, is the divine Prototype. Insofar as his opened side gives birth not only to his spouse as in Adam, but also to the children of God, his death casts him in the role of a woman in labour. Considered in this light, the glory of the suffering in John becomes immediately clear: it is the pain of parturition, over which one's family does not agonise but joyfully accepts.

The figure indeed was in Jesus' mind shortly before his suffering began for, thinking about his disciples' anguish at his parting, he encouraged them thus: 'when a woman is in travail she has sorrow, because her hour has come; but when she is delivered of the child, she no longer remembers the anguish, for joy that a child is born into the world. So you have sorrow now, but I will see you again and your hearts will rejoice, and no one will take your joy from you' (John 16:21–22).

They had already experienced the truth of his words, long before the Gospel came to be written. It was in the era of that joy that the Passion was re-told, in the aura of post-natal jubilation that his death was described. After the Apostolic period the earliest commentators on the text picked up its full theological implication. St John Chrysostom again, in the homily cited earlier, continues:

> Have you seen with what kind of food he [Christ] feeds us all? By the same food we are formed and are fed. As a woman feeds her child with her own blood and milk, so too Christ himself continually feeds those whom he has begotten with his own blood. (*To Catechumens*, chapter 3)

The breast-feeding Christ is a very daring interpretation. But no more so than that of him giving birth. In our own time Pope John Paul II provides a reasoned basis for considering the extremely explicit Johannine imagery of Jesus' maternity. Taking account of the Old Testament passages on God's motherly love (texts which we have already looked at in the section on Luke's Passion), he finds in Biblical anthropomorphic language a way of pointing indirectly to 'the mystery of the eternal "generating" which belongs to the inner life of God' (*On the Dignity and Vocation of Women*, §8). Generating however, he explains, is neither exclusively masculine nor feminine; it is both. Hebrew literature may have attributed male parenthood to the Godhead but since God is not man or woman, motherhood is as equally valid a category to describe the divine begetting as fatherhood is.

> In itself this 'generating' (within the Trinity) has neither 'masculine' nor 'feminine' qualities. It is by nature totally divine. It is spiritual in the most perfect way, since "God is spirit" (Jn 4:24) and possesses no property typical of the body, neither 'feminine' nor 'masculine'. Thus even 'fatherhood' in God is completely divine and free of the 'masculine' bodily characteristics proper to human fatherhood. . . .
>
> Although it is not possible to attribute human qualities to the eternal generation of the Word of God, and although the divine fatherhood does not possess 'masculine' characteristics in a physical sense, we must nevertheless seek in God the absolute model of all 'generation' among human beings. . . . All 'generating' among creatures finds its primary model in that generating which in God is completely divine, that is, spiritual. . . . Thus every element of human generation which is proper to man, and every element which is proper to woman, namely human 'fatherhood' and 'motherhood', bears within itself a likeness to, or analogy with the divine 'generating' and with that 'fatherhood' which in God is totally different – that is, completely spiritual and divine in essence.
>
> (*On the Dignity and Vocation of Women*, §8)

Given that divine generation within the Trinity is above and beyond human parenthood, is the source from which all fatherhood (and motherhood) on earth is derived (Eph. 3:14–15) and therefore transcends our gender descriptions of it, it is not inappropriate to think of the crucified Christ as

Mother, just as it is not inappropriate to address God as our Father. This is not to negate the manhood of the historical Jesus (as we saw in the last chapter), nor to dilute the integrity of his maleness. What it means is that we do not circumscribe his work and glory within the narrow confines of our cultural perspectives. The Paschal Mystery after all is greater in its significance than we can cope with: no expression of its salvific impact is an exaggeration.

We belong to a tradition that has often dared to step out of conventional self-expression to grasp the fecundity of God. The seventh-century Council of Toledo for instance – a very local affair comprising only seventeen bishops, largely forgotten today but whose statement on the Trinity is simply magnificent – dared to describe the consubstantiality of the Second Person with the First in terms of feminine procreation: 'We must believe that the Son is begotten or born . . . *from the womb of the Father*, that is from His substance' (The Eleventh Council of Toledo: *Symbol of Faith*, AD 675). With regards Christ's maternity, medieval Christian spirituality was no less forthright. Aelred de Rievaulx (died 1167) speaks of Christ nourishing the recluse with milk as a mother does (*De institutione inclusarum*), while the Ancrene Riwle (a thirteenth-century Rule for contemplatives) even depicts him as a mother playing with her children, consoling and washing them.

But the apex of this spiritual tradition undoubtedly is to be found in the Revelations of Divine Love to Julian of Norwich (1342–1416). Her meditation on the theme is prolonged and repeated. Between chapters 58 and 64 inclusive she examines the idea from the personal point of view and the ecclesial-sacramental. In chapter 60 she combines both, recapitulating the best of the Patristics and the essence of the Johannine symbolism and signs.

The human mother will suckle her child with her own milk, but our beloved Mother, Jesus, feeds us with himself, and with the most tender courtesy, does it by means of the Blessed Sacrament, the precious food of all true life. And he keeps us going through his mercy and grace by all the sacraments. . . . The human mother may put her child tenderly to her breast, but our tender Mother Jesus simply leads us into his blessed breast through his open side, and there he gives us a glimpse of the God-head and heavenly joy – the inner certainty of eternal bliss.*

What Julian is describing, albeit in the most personal terminology, is that communion with Christ in word and sacrament which the Church of the Fourth Gospel saw as the terminus of their faith and the purpose of their witness to others. The origin of the breast-feeding motif, which peaks at the crucifixion, is the Last Supper, with the Beloved Disciple leaning his head against Jesus. Their intimate table-fellowship is proudly recorded no less than three times – clearly an important and cherished memory for the Johannine Church. Notably because it underlined the special place held by their Founding Member in the Lord's affections. But no less because it specified the Apostolic charism by which they identified themselves as an ecclesial community.

One of his disciples, whom Jesus loved, was lying close to the breast of Jesus. . . . So lying thus, close to the breast of Jesus, he said to him, 'Lord, who is it (who will betray you)?'. . . Peter turned and saw following them the disciple whom Jesus loved, who had lain close to his breast at the

*Penguin translation by C. Wolters, 1976, p. 170.

194

supper and had said, 'Lord, who is it that is going to betray you?' (John 13:23, 25; 21:20)

In his homilies on John's Gospel, St Augustine refers to this scene (and the relationship it stands for) as the source of the extraordinary vision of the Fourth Gospel. He does so in language that is strongly reminiscent of the suckling child. 'For the sake of the faithful, in order to preserve the still and secret heart of the next life, John the Evangelist rested on Christ's breast.... John drank from the well of the Lord's breast knowledge of the Word, who in the beginning was God and with God, and all else concerning Christ's divinity – sublime knowledge proclaimed by John concerning the trinity and unity of the whole godhead, which in his kingdom we shall see face to face' (Homily 124).

Moreover, because the context of the leaning is the Supper table, the suckling is not only of the Word as wisdom, but of the Blood as communion. So important was the Sacrament together with the teaching, the evangelist devoted an entire chapter of his text to Jesus' eucharistic discourse. Christ's own words would explain best the significance of the feeding from his body which the Meal would bequeath in mystery and the cross would accomplish in fact.

> 'Truly, truly, I say to you, unless you eat the flesh of the Son of Man and drink his blood, you have no life in you; he who eats my flesh and drinks my blood has eternal life, and I will raise him up at the last day. For my flesh is food indeed, and my blood is drink indeed. He who eats my flesh and drinks my blood abides in me, and I in him.'
>
> (John 6:53–56)

The discourse comes directly after those chapters on the theme of water and rebirth: Jesus' conversation with Nicodemus whose astonishment that one must be born anew to enter the kingdom prompted the question, 'How can a man be born when he is old? Can he enter a second time into his mother's womb and be born?' (3:4); the mass baptisms for repentance at which Jesus' disciples assisted (3:22; 4:1–2); the offer of living water to the woman at the well (4:7–15); and the healing of the disabled man at the waters of Bethzatha in Jerusalem (5:1–9). It is followed by the great cry of Jesus at the feast of Tabernacles in chapter 7 when on the last day of the celebrations 'he stood up and proclaimed, "If any one thirst, let him come to me and drink. He who believes in me, as the scripture has said, Out of his heart shall flow rivers of living water" ' (vv. 37–38), a reference to the Spirit 'which those who believed in him were to receive' (v. 39).

Thus the very structure of the text reflects the synthesis of birth and breast-feeding, water and blood, re-generation and nourishment, that constitutes the divine maternity of Christ. That maternity runs through the whole of his ministry, emerging through the signs, touching the many who believed in him.

Indeed the entire account of Christ's life and death is held together at its public beginning and triumphant end by the two signs that abbreviate and synopsise the meaning of Jesus for the community of the Beloved Disciple. At Cana in Galilee he turned water into wine for the marriage feast, symbol of the messianic banquet; at Calvary he poured out the wine, now turned to blood, from the chalice of his flesh. The emphasis on this pouring replaces in John the words of institution at the Last Supper which the synoptics include. This evangelist's disciples were already familiar with those words; they needed no reminder of them. Instead he left them his own personal eye-witness account of what the words meant, his graphic description of the glorious motherhood of the kingly Saviour pierced.

Although the maternity of Christ is represented in the synoptic tradition, it is treated differently in John. In Luke it takes the form of compassion for sinners and adds to the poignancy of the sacrifice willingly endured. In the Fourth Gospel however it brings out the powerful efficiency with which Jesus dealt with evil. His femininity is no fragile matter. It has all the instinct determination and force of a mother defending that to which she has given life, a force to be reckoned with. Such instinct cares little for its own survival, making it, even in the natural world, particularly dangerous.

Something of that holy ferocity in Christ comes out through the course of his confrontation with 'the Jews'. In his uncompromising defence of the truth, for example, his detestation of lies and deceit, his open lack of sympathy with sham religiosity, his utter condemnation of sin. Even with his own disciples he did not shirk directness. 'Jesus answered them, "Did I not choose you, the twelve, and one of you is a devil?" ' (6:70). And to those whom he had healed and pardoned, 'Sin no more, that nothing worse befall you' (5:14). But particularly with his public opponents, who threatened all that he strove to achieve for his children in terms of eternal life, his speech was a naked sword. 'I go away, and you will seek me and die in your sin; where I am going, you cannot come' (8:21); 'You are of your father the devil, and your will is to do your father's desires' (8:44); 'Jesus said, "For judgment I came into this world, that those who do not see may see, and that those who see may become blind". Some of the Pharisees near him heard this, and they said to him, "Are we also blind?" Jesus said to them, "If you were blind, you would have no guilt; but now that you say, 'We see', your guilt remains" ' (9:39–41).

Even when a mother sees that her death is inevitable for her offspring to be saved she will continue to protect them to the end. So it was with Jesus. Calm in the face of his own arrest, he nonetheless sheltered his followers. Like a shrewd decoy drawing an enemy's attention away from its young, 'Jesus answered [the soldiers], "I told you that I am he; so, if you seek me, let these men go". This was to fulfil the word which he had spoken, "Of those whom you gave me I lost not one" ' (18:8–9). It was a speech familiar to his lips; he had used it more than once before. 'Let her alone', he ordered the one who accused Mary of Bethany at the anointing; and for the sake of her brother Lazarus whom he raised from the dead he commanded the on-lookers, 'Unbind him, and let him go' (12:7, and 11:44 respectively).

The strength of this love is consistent. It never varies, it never weakens. If necessary it submits to death in child-birth, even scorning death's gloating for the sake of life's gain. This kind of motherhood is in line with the vigorous child-bearers of the Old Testament tradition. It began with the Hebrew women in Egypt who resisted Pharaoh's attempts to extermi-nate their male progeny. Despite his dictatorship he was defeated both by the pregnant and the midwives.

The midwives feared God and did not do as the king of Egypt commanded them, but let the male children live. So the king of Egypt called the midwives, and said to them, 'Why have you done this, and let the male children live?' The midwives said to Pharaoh, 'Because the Hebrew women are not like the Egyptian women; for they are vigorous and are delivered before the midwife comes to them'. So God dealt well with the midwives; and the people multiplied and grew very strong. And because the midwives feared God he gave them families.

(Exod. 1:17–22)

It ends with the mother of seven sons in the Second Book of the Maccabees who so cared for their spiritual welfare that she watched each one tortured and put to death by the impious Greeks before submitting to the same fate herself (7:1–42).

Biblical motherhood therefore is about preserving life and sacrificing it, and sacrificing it in order to restore it. Which is why the woman in Second Maccabees encouraged her sons to stand firm in the face of trial against apostasy: 'Accept death,' she urged her youngest, 'so that in God's mercy I may get you back again with your brothers' (7:29). This requires a different kind of vigour from purely physical strength. Throughout the udaeo-Christian tradition there have always been women of real moral muscle, Amazons capable of leading the nation to integrity and self-respect. Deborah from the Book of Judges, Abigail who averted the wrath of David, Esther among the exiles who saved the Jews from annihilation. After Christ, Brigid of Ireland, Jeanne d'Arc, Catherine of Siena and the great St Teresa. All of them mighty figures who transformed the contours of history for the good and were revered as matriarchs in the society or Church where their influence was felt.

In the community of John too there is evidence that strong women contributed to the growth of faith and were held in high regard. According to the Fourth Gospel many of them played a pivotal role in the narrative of Jesus. One prompted the start of his messianic work before its time (2:4–5); another brought an entire township to its faith-encounter with him

(4:39); two received the revelation of his Christ-identity which in the synoptics was reserved for Peter and the Eleven (John 4:25–26; 11:27); one discovered him to be 'the resurrection and the life' (11:25), and another was the first witness to his resurrection and first to announce it to the Apostles (20:16, 18). In each case a key event, a major turning-point that bore fruit, involved the vital and vigorous participation of the feminine with whom he shared the mystery of his powerful, life-giving force.

Clearly this is an advance even from the Lucan tradition. There the participation was more passive than active. Here it is dynamic, authoritative, kerygmatic and almost sacramental. These women reverse the folly of Eve. They are the Church as Mother. Not because they are strong in themselves, for each was either poor, or sinful or wretched or possessed, and all were without status in Hebrew or Samaritan society; but because by their association with Christ they came to embody his maternity in the work he gave them to do.

If Christ is the true Eve, mothering all who live, he is even more explicitly for John the true Moses, for Moses too was a mother figure who shared his maternal burden with others capable of helping him. When the children of Israel grumbled in the desert at the manna provided for them – the ancestors of those who rejected the true bread from heaven offered by Jesus in John chapter 6 – the Patriarch laid his frustration before the Lord with all the despair of a mother who has lost control of her family.

> Moses said to the Lord, 'Why have you dealt ill with your servant . . . that you lay the burden of all this people upon me? Did I conceive all this people? Did I bring them forth, that you should say to me, "Carry them in your bosom, as

the nurse carries the sucking child".... I am not able to carry all this people alone, the burden is too heavy for me.'

(Num. 11: 11–14)

Not alone did Moses carry his people like a mother carries her child, bearing the burden of them. He also fed them with bread as a mother does when they were hungry and gave them fresh water to drink when they were parched. In every instance John the evangelist understood these signs as lights that illuminated the works of Jesus. But none more so than the sign of the bronze serpent.

The snake in scripture, as in the whole of ancient near-Eastern culture, evokes an ambivalent response. On the one hand its bite brings death; on the other its serum brings healing. Among the pagan peoples it was a fertility symbol, celebrating life; among the monotheistic Hebrews its cult was idolatrous. In one shaft of light it was evil, in another shaft it was holy.

Because the children of Israel continued to grumble even after they had been fed, 'the Lord sent fiery serpents among the people, and they bit the people so that many people of Israel died' (Num. 21:6). The serpent here is a symbol of death. It mirrors the horror in Eden when the innocent Eve actually conversed with the reptile, unaware of the mortal danger of its hypnotic spell. Slowly uncoiling its false arguments, slithering subtly around her unprotected naivety, its venomous strike is sudden and sure. And so it would be for all who disregard the word of God in preference for the promptings of Satan. The offspring of Eve would always be vulnerable before the serpent and the diabolical moral threat it represented. 'I will put enmity between you and the woman,' God told the serpent, 'and between your seed and her seed . . . and you shall bruise his heel' (Gen. 3:15).

When the fiery serpents struck again at the children of Eve in the wilderness beyond Eden, a physical affliction caused by and signifying their inner state of pride and disobedience (1 Cor. 10:9–11), Moses interceded for them and they were healed. 'The Lord said to Moses, "Make a fiery serpent, and set it on a pole; and everyone who is bitten, when he sees it, shall live." So Moses made a bronze serpent, and set it on a pole; and if a serpent bit any man, he would look at the bronze serpent and live' (Num. 21:8–9). The serpent here is a symbol of salvation.

If Moses stands therefore in contradistinction to Eve, healing by his fertile fidelity what Eve by careless neglect exposed to attack, he is not for all that the Messiah. His maternal intercession did not restore Israel, still less his snake-effigy. As the Book of Wisdom pointed out, 'When your people, Lord, were being destroyed by the bites of writhing serpents . . . and received a token of deliverance . . . he who turned towards it was saved, not by what he saw, but by you, the Saviour of all' (16:5–7). Or as the Letter to the Hebrews put it, 'Moses was faithful in all God's house as a servant, to testify to the things that were to be spoken later, but Christ was faithful over God's house as a son', and therefore 'Jesus has been counted worthy of as much more glory than Moses as a builder of a house has more honour than the house' (3:5, 3).

The glory of Moses' bronze token was destroyed five centuries later by Hezekiah the King as part of his religious reform, 'for until those days the people of Israel had burned incense to it' (2 Kings 18:4). The glory it prefigured however, was itself to destroy the worship of anything but God himself. This glory, of which Jesus was counted worthy, would irrad-

icate the corruption that even religion was not exempt from.
It would fulfil the deliverance from the fangs of evil and the
bite of death that the Book of Wisdom said belonged to God
alone, and of which Moses' deliverance was but a promissory
shadow. For the writer of the Fourth Gospel shadow gives way
to light in the exaltation of the cross.

> As Moses lifted up the serpent in the wilderness [Jesus
> said to Nicodemus], so must the Son of man be lifted up,
> that whoever believes in him may have eternal life.
> (3:14–15)

Here was the authentic healing that only divine motherhood
can achieve, greater than the medicine of Moses, more life-
giving than the womb of Eve. Not made of bronze, but radiant
with grace. Not fiery like the inflamation caused by venom,
but aflame in the flesh of the crucified king. Not elevated on a
standard in the desert, but enthroned on the wood of the cross.
Not bringing temporary reprieve from the grave, but eternal
life. Not inviting indifferent observation, but attracting the
eye of faith along the upward gaze of hope.

'You will strike its heel,' God had told the serpent concerning Eve's offspring, 'but it will crush your head' (Gen.
3:15. JB). To do so he would have to leave his heel vulnerable
to the venom. And for that he became worthy of the glory.
Standing in for Israel he was bitten; bitten, he died the death
of Everyman; dying, he crushed the head of death itself; and
being lifted up he was made the means of healing for all. For
in John the 'lifting up' always has a double significance. It
refers initially to the raising of the cross-beam, but equally and
simultaneously to the resurrection and to the ascension by
which he returned in his humanity to the Father whom he
never left in his divinity.

The glory of Christ however is not deferred until the latter phases of the mystery are accomplished. It is fully contained in the crucifixion itself. Just as Calvary was also the moment of the outpouring of the Spirit in John, so too out of Calvary comes the rising and ascending. The second up-lifting is one with the first. Good Friday holds in its womb already the seeds of Easter Day. So when Jesus likened himself to the serpent in the wilderness he was thinking first of his cross, but always in the light of its consequence: resurrection and life eternal.

Christ's words to Nicodemus are repeated three times throughout John's account of the Good News. To the hostile Jews in chapter 8, 'Jesus said, "When you have lifted up the Son of man, then *you will know* that I am he"' (v. 25); and to the crowd standing near him in chapter 12 he completed the import of his meaning: 'And I, when I am lifted up from the earth, *will draw all men* to myself' (v. 32).

Three times through the course of Jesus' life John keeps the serpent image before our eyes: at the beginning, the middle and the end. It punctuates his narrative at its crossing points, leading us step by step to the full meaning of the triumphant elevation of the king. The cross is glorious because as well as inviting the faith that saves, it actually causes it. So to Nicodemus was revealed its reliability as the sign that men can believe in; to the Jews was given the reason why: this sign will establish the divine identity of the one who restores life through it – 'You will know that I am he'; and to the crowds on the third occasion was announced the effect that the sign will produce, namely unity. 'I will draw all men to myself'.

The context in each case is the contrasting lack of faith, a sable backdrop against which the Crucified burns like beaten bronze. Dissension was always part of the serpent story – from the murmuring of the Hebrews which caused the fiery image to be fashioned in the first place, to their perverted worship of the thing, treating it as an end in itself rather than as a type of the deeper healing that was to come.

As then, so now. Nicodemus, the leading Pharisee who came to Christ by night, was keen enough to talk about religion, but no witness moved him to commitment. Neither that of the Baptist whose voice proclaimed Jesus as Lamb of God and messianic bridegroom (in the chapters before and after Nicodemus' visit), nor the voice of the Johannine community whose testimony to Jesus' words and works echoed the testimony of the Father and Jesus together: 'Truly, truly, I say to you, we speak of what we know, and bear witness to what we have seen; but you do not receive our testimony' (3:11). This man was that which is born of the flesh, not that which is born of the Spirit. He did not understand even the earthly things of Jesus' teaching. How then was he to understand the heavenly?

Similarly with the hostile Jews of chapter 8. 'You are from below', Jesus said to them, 'I am from above; you are of this world, I am not of this world' (v. 23). They refused to believe in the one 'who sent me' (v. 26), therefore could not grasp who Jesus was (v. 25), nor recognise that the witness to him was not just his own but the Father's as well (v. 18). They preferred to cling to Moses and the Law, the feasts and sacrifices of the Temple worship, idolising the physical types instead of the saving reality as their fathers had done before them. Earlier in the Prologue John had made this very clear. 'Though the Law was given through Moses, grace and truth have come through Jesus Christ' and yet, ironically, 'his own people did not accept him' (1:17, 11. JB) for 'though the light has come into the world men have shown they prefer darkness to the light' (3:19. JB).

By chapter 12 the darkness is deepening. It is the eve of his passion. Already the April light is fading, the late afternoon is sultry and thundery (vv. 29, 35–36). The tension increases between the coming judgement and their stubborn refusal to accept the offer of grace. Jesus urges them to act. It is the last time he will do so for soon he will be dead. ' "Walk while you have the light, lest the darkness overtake you; he who walks in the darkness does not know where he goes. . . . While you have the light, believe in the light, that you may become sons of light". . . . Jesus cried out and said . . . "I have come as light into the world, that whoever believes in me may not remain in darkness. . . . He who rejects me and does not receive my sayings has a judge; the word that I have spoken will be his judge on the last day" ' (vv. 35–36, 44, 46, 48).

For all these words, for all his signs, no response. Standing by, watching and witnessing, the evangelist expresses his utter amazement. 'Yet they did not believe in him. . . . Therefore they could not believe . . . [though] many of the authorities did believe in him, for fear of the Pharisees they did not confess it . . . they loved the praise of men more than the praise of God' (12:37, 39, 42–43).

Even more amazing is that despite the resistance to him, Jesus' prophecy remains firmly in place, raised like a standard in their midst, thrice repeated: 'And I, when I am lifted up, will draw all men to myself; then you will know that I am he; the Son of man must be lifted up as Moses lifted up the serpent in the wilderness'. It bears all the calm assurance and confidence of his kingliness, shows the same inner strength and control of circumstance that he showed at his trial. Somehow – though John never resolves the mystery of it either in his Letters or in his Gospel – the reign of God is being established in exact accordance with the plan. Not despite the opposition, but through it.

Therefore, 'All shall be well,' and 'all manner of things shall be well,' as Julian of Norwich put it, quoting Christ's revelation to her, though she could not see how, given that men are free to reject him (*Revelations of Divine Love*, chapter 32). Yet if the Jews had not rejected Jesus he would not have been crucified. There would have been no resurrection, no glory. In St Paul's words, 'If Christ has not been raised, your faith is futile and you are still in your sins. Then those also who have fallen asleep in Christ have perished. If for this life only we have hoped in Christ, we are of all men most to be pitied' (1 Cor. 15:17–18).

In his humanity Jesus resolutely faces the rejection, the failure to convince his own people, the betrayal by Judas, his impeachment, his fate. For one brief instant John allows an echo of the mental agony depicted by the synoptics. 'Now is my soul troubled' (12:27). He does so only to show, from Jesus' subsequent speech, his conscious re-commitment to God's will at the very onset of distress. 'And what shall I say? "Father, save me from this hour"? No, for this purpose I have come to this hour. Father, glorify your name' (vv. 27–28).

At this precise moment the Father's voice responds audibly from heaven. 'I have glorified it, and I will glorify it again' (12:28). Not, as in the other Gospels, 'This is my Beloved Son', for throughout the entire course of John, the writer has made the beloved relationship between Christ and his Father very clear. Did not Christ say more than once, 'I and the Father are one'; 'The Father is in me and I am in the Father'; 'The Father loves the Son, and shows him all that he himself is doing'; and 'He who sent me is with me . . . for I always do what is pleasing to him' (John 10:30; 38; 5:20; 8:28 respectively)?

Nor does John place the Father's voice at the beginning of his Gospel at the Jordan river, for in John there is no account of Jesus' baptism. Nor does the voice come in the middle of his Gospel on Mount Tabor, for in John there is no transfiguration. It comes rather on the very threshold of the passion. The writer focuses all the glory on the cross itself, not the events which prefigured it, unlike Mark, Matthew and Luke whose radiant theophanies anticipated the splendour of crucified love, but removed it to a respectful distance from the scandalous sacrilege that also was Golgotha.

What John does give us in this scene is direct access to the loving conversation between the First and Second Person of the Godhead. This is no monologue from on high resounding on the waters of a river or the peak of a mountain. It is the intimate dialogue between the eternal Father and the pre-existent Son, made public for one split second, like a rattle of thunder – enough to grant us insight into their perfect communion of mind and will. In the brief exchange between the Messiah and the One who sent him – brief but containing the infinite fulness of eternity – the startling fact is, they are speaking about *us*. Their subject is sacrifice; their objective, to gather up all humanity into the glorious inner life and joy of divine love.

Nor is this conversation like the one recorded in St Luke between Jesus and Moses and Elijah at the transfiguration when 'they spoke of his departure [his death], which he was to accomplish at Jerusalem' (Luke 9:31). There the Old Testament heroes could add nothing to what they had said already about the mystery in figure, through Law and prophecy. Here however John lifts the veil that shrouds the mystery, letting us glimpse the cross at the very heart of God's love for his Son and the Son's love for the Father and their one love for the world.

'This voice has come for your sake,' Jesus told the crowd, 'not for mine' (John 12:30). We were meant to hear it. It was a revelation to explain revelation itself. The intention was not to inspire dread like the thunder-clap at Sinai (Exod. 19:16; 20:18–20), but gratitude. As the Letter to the Hebrews (so close in many of its themes to the Johannine corpus) would later explain:

> You have not come to . . . the sound of a trumpet, and a voice whose words made the hearers entreat that no further messages be spoken to them. . . . But you have come to Mount Zion and to the city of the living God, the heavenly Jerusalem . . . and to the assembly of the first-born who are enrolled in heaven . . . and to Jesus, the mediator of a new covenant, and to the sprinkled blood that speaks more graciously than the blood of Abel. See that you do not refuse him who is speaking . . . (but) let us be grateful for receiving a kingdom that cannot be shaken, and thus let us offer to God acceptable worship, with reverence and awe.
> (12:18–28)

Only they could render thanks who actually heard the voice. Not all present did. Some thought it *was* thunder, others that an angel had spoken (John 12:29). Earlier Jesus had reproached the Jews who had not listened to him, 'The Father who sent me has himself borne witness to me. His voice you have never heard, his form you have never seen; and you do not have his word abiding in you' (John 5:37–38). But to those who did believe in him, his own apostles, he explained the meaning of the voice, showed the reason for gratitude in the Priestly Prayer he offered for them and the Church as his last will and testament before going to his death.

'I have glorified [my name],' said the Father's voice from heaven. It was the gospel truth. Jesus was that name, God's own identity, his perfect definition; by God's power his time on earth had been all a glorification of the Father, an exquisite hymn of praise which he had taught his disciples. The canticle of his life he had given to them that they might know the One who sings it for it was the Father's love-song calling them to himself.

> This is eternal life, that they may know you the only true God and Jesus Christ whom you have sent. I glorified you on earth, having accomplished the work which you gave me to do. . . . I have manifested your name to the men whom you gave me out of the world . . . and they have kept your word. . . . While I was with them, I kept them in your name, which you have given me.
>
> (John 17:3–4, 6, 12)

As obedient Son and kingly Messiah he now prays that all he has done may return to the Father and be crowned with his glory.

'I have glorified it, and I will glorify it again,' the voice assured him. The work would return to him, would be crowned through its last, stunning manifestation of the Son's goodness, the evening oblation of thanksgiving and praise from Calvary. And so Jesus affirms, 'For their sake I consecrate [in John the word means to sacrifice] myself, that they also may be consecrated in truth' (17:18).

The cross is the ultimate truth about God and man. Through the cross all will be consecrated – both the apostles and those who through their word will come to believe in

Christ; for through the cross all enter into the oneness of the Trinity.

> Holy Father, keep them in your name . . . that they may be one, even as we are one . . . [I pray] that they may all be one; even as you, Father, are in me, and I in you, that they also may be in us, so that the world may believe that you have sent me. . . . That they may be one even as we are one, I in them and you in me, that they may become perfectly one. (John 17:11, 21–23)

It was for the unity of his followers that Christ died – their unity among themselves achieved by their unity with him, and through him with the Father. What Christ had in mind was not some general consensus of like-minded people. He intended a profound communion of heart and will in his Church; a living organism that would think and breathe and live in rhythm with the Triune Godhead; a communion in faith and worship based on a life of personal integrity like his own, arising from a pure heart and undefiled conscience.

The other name for unity is holiness. And so he also prayed, 'Sanctify them in the truth' (17:17). In other words, Make them holy as God is holy. This is why he chose to describe their unity in terms of his own oneness with the Father. 'May they be one even as we are one'. It is the most daring line in scripture. Had anyone said it other than Jesus it would have been blasphemy. Which is why the Pharisees were so taken aback by him.

To suggest that men could attain the holy unity of God is incredible. It is to suggest that we might become 'perfect as your heavenly Father is perfect' (Matt. 5:48). It is to imply that we could 'become partakers of the divine nature' (2 Pet. 1:4), could become God himself. And yet this is precisely what

Jesus meant. It would require such a transformation that one would have to think of it as the emergence of new life from within, like branches growing out of a vine. That too is what Jesus was thinking of. 'I am the vine', he told them, 'you are the branches. He who abides in me, and I in him, he it is that bears much fruit' (John 15:5).

One thing alone could make this possible. Not the efforts of men, for even the idea of what Jesus proposed was unimaginable. Only the personal prayer of Jesus to God and God's personal response to that prayer would do. By Love's invitation alone might men enter into Love's holy communion which is the fulness of life. Because that prayer ended with the sign of the cross, it was granted. Indeed the very presence of Jesus on earth was a sign that the intention which inspired it was an eternal intention, uttered and answered even before time began now revealed in time that it might be fulfilled in reality.

> May they become perfectly one, so that the world may know that . . . you have loved them even as you have loved me. Father, I desire that they also, whom you have given me, may be with me where I am, to behold my glory which you have given me in your love for me before the foundation of the world. O righteous Father. . . . I made known to them your name, and I will make it known, that the love with which you have loved me may be in them, and I in them. (John 17:23–26)

It is the climax of the entire discourse. The love of God for man has been paralleled with the love of God for God. The Father's love for the world is as great as his love for the Son. The Holy Spirit of that love cannot be divided. When it is given it is given completely. He cannot love more or less. The same love which is the bond of unity between the Voice and the Word, which is the very essence of the divine nature, now includes the creature whom he made. For him to renege on this would be to deny himself; would be for the Father to cease loving his Beloved Son, for the Son to cease loving his Beloved Father, which could never be. Mankind's destiny is to be lifted up into the eternal generation of the Son from the Father, into the Love that proceeds from both so perfectly that it makes the three Persons one God.

The very structure of the Priestly Prayer reflects the mystery. Composed of complementary ideas set out in parallel, it is chiastic in form (from the shape of the Greek letter, *chi*, written like our capital X). The first idea is paralleled with the last in a section, the second paralleled with the second-last and so on, till those above converge with those below at the intersection of the X. In each case while the ideas paired are thematically the same, something new emerges from the one below that enhances the thought expressed without taking anything away from the one above or adding anything to it substantially different.

Among the themes paired and paralleled: that those who believe might bring the world to believe; through their unity which reflects the unity of God himself; that they might see the glory of the Son – already revealed through the word – as the glory which he had from before the beginning of the world; this glory which is the love between the Father and the Son and is now given to men through their faith in Christ.

The interplay of these ideas, which can also be likened to concentric circles or even spirals moving in and out of one another, are reminiscent of the generation and procession within the Three-Personed God. Nothing is added, nothing diminished from the one substance revealed. Yet the Word goes forth from the Father and returns to him again taking with him all humankind; the Spirit of love goes forth from the Father and the Son and returns having sanctified the world. Thus even in the inspired composition of the passage the idea of the Church is intrinsically blended with the idea of the Trinity so that it is difficult to separate Jesus' words about God from his words about us. Already his promise has come true: 'When I am lifted up from the earth I will draw all men to myself'.

It is through the cross that the promise is realised, the glory shared.

In John that cross is a bejewelled spectacle of incredible beauty, God's royal sceptre, the escutcheon of his kingdom. It is like the crosses of the Middle Ages where the wounds were rubies mounted on gold, the blood from his side pure amethyst, the crown on his head bright pearl, all diamonds for tears. So ornate that they had to be covered up in purple during Lent so that Christendom could concentrate on the pain. It was the glory of the cross that the Anglo-Saxon poet first recalled in the account of his 'Dream of the Rood', cited earlier.

> I perceived a strange and lovely tree,
> Most radiant, rising up before me
> Surrounded by light; it was clothed
> In gleaming gold; five precious jewels
> Studded its cross-beam and many more were strewn
> Around it on the earth. All the angels of the Lord
>   protected it,
> Created so fair. That was no cross of a malefactor,
> But holy spirits and men of this earth
> Watched over it there . . . the entire universe.

(lines 4–12)

As long ago as the Middle Ages art captured the meaning of John – and as recently as Salvador Dali in his vision of the crucifixion from above. For there, taking the Father's perspective, the body of Christ is all light. Not just reflecting the surrealist light of an evening sun, but generating light of its own from a corpse as intact as that of a lamb without blemish.

If all these, following John, translate pain into beauty, darkness into glory, defeat into victory, the Fourth Gospel nevertheless leaves us with one figure at its Calvary for whom this death could only have been pure anguish. Though silent like the Father, the Mother of Jesus stood by his cross to the end, her emotions left strangely unrecorded – perhaps out of respect. Apart from God himself, to her alone belonged the words: 'This is my Son, the Beloved'. Though not attributed to her lips they were undoubtedly spoken in her heart as she held him in her arms before they laid him in the tomb.

Excursus:
Mother of the Beloved

UNLIKE THE SYNOPTICS, John clearly records the presence at Calvary of the Mother of Jesus and the disciple whom Jesus loved. Close to the heart of the Crucified they stand at the foot of the cross in mystical communion with the Word made flesh, caught up through suffering in the ineffable love between Father and Son. They are the first fruits of Jesus' promise to draw all things to himself when he is lifted up from the earth; first fruits of his prayer that all might be one as he and the Father are one.

And yet neither of them is named, here or elsewhere in the Fourth Gospel. Their role in the plan for the glorification of the world will be their identity in the Church that proclaims this Gospel. Already it requires of them to leave aside their natural ties of affection for him as Son, as bosom companion. Henceforth they will know him at a deeper, spiritual level as the Messiah-King and Lord of the Universe.

In this new and disorienting relationship they are first among those Jesus described as 'from above . . . not of this world' (John 8:23), who therefore view the cross from above, not from below. But if their proclamation of Calvary is to be life for others it must also be a transforming faith experience for them as witnesses. The cost will be their full participation in his pain, the loss of him whom they love, and the dispossession of all they once were to him that they might become what he now wishes them to be. In his last moments on the cross he reveals the place he has prepared for them in his new creation, 'that they might be with me where I am' (John 17:24).

> When Jesus saw his mother, and the disciple whom he loved standing near, he said to his mother, 'Woman, behold your son!' Then he said to the disciple, 'Behold, your mother!' And from that moment the disciple took her to his home. (John 19:26–27)

For Mary these are words that lance the soul. She who was honoured to have been Mother of the Beloved Son is now asked to be Mother of the Beloved Disciple instead. The poignancy of her situation was sensitively considered by the twelfth-century Cistercian, Bernard of Clairvaux:

> 'Mother, behold your son.' These words were more painful than a sword thrust for they touched the quick where soul is divided from spirit. What an exchange! John was given to you in place of Jesus, a disciple in place of the Master, a son of Zebedee in place of the Son of God, a mere man in place of the true God. These words must have pierced your loving soul, since just to recall them breaks our hearts, hard and stony though they be. (Sermon 14)

It would mean for her, as it would later mean for Paul, a radical change of perspective. 'From now on, therefore, we regard no one from a human point of view; even though we once regarded Christ from a human point of view, we regard him thus no longer' (2 Cor. 5:16).

To find the Son she has lost she must look for him in the

disciple. And not only in John but in all the faithful, whom he represents. She will be Mother to them as she has been to Christ; for they, the Church, are now his body. If she would reign with the King of love on Calvary, she must serve those he is drawing to himself, as he served them by yielding up his Spirit.

> In this Mary became the first of those who 'serving Christ also in others with humility and patience lead their brothers and sisters to that King whom to serve is to reign', and she fully obtained that 'state of royal freedom' proper to Christ's disciples: to serve means to reign! (John Paul II, *Redemptoris Mater*, §41, citing Vatican II's *Lumen gentium*, §36)

At Calvary Mary too yielded up her spirit, her natural claim over the offspring of her womb and all the rights that go with it. She sacrificed the possessive instinct of exclusive motherly love that it might be transformed into the fulness and maturity of universal Motherhood in the order of grace.

The other Gospels had already dealt with the question of Jesus' attitude towards his blood-relatives as one who preached a kingdom of repentance and faith, and their status in that kingdom as his kinsmen. The synoptics made it clear that no privilege attached to carnal bonds with the Saviour. Salvation belongs to those alone who relate to him in spirit. This applied equally to the Virgin Mary. She was blessed not just because of genetics, but because she believed (Luke 1:45), because she pondered the word and treasured it in her heart (Luke 2:19; 33; 51), and because she heard the will of God and did it (Luke 1:38; Mark 3:35). By the time the last Gospel came to be written, the point had been well aired. Now it was time to set down what the Beloved Disciple had handed on to the

Johannine community of Mary's part in the glorious triumph of her redeeming Son, as Mother not only of the Redeemer but also of the Redeemed.

Golgotha marks the apex of the strong and vigorous motherhood of Jesus: the parturition of the Church, conceived in the womb of the Trinity, now emerging in the blood and water from his side as he gives up his life in child-birth. By defining Mary's new spiritual motherhood before he dies, he entrusts his whole Mystical Body to her maternal solicitude as once he abandoned his physical body into her care at Bethlehem: that Mystical Body which itself will bring forth and nourish future generations of citizens for the Kingdom.

As well as engaging her personal co-operation in this regard therefore, he also makes her the model and sign of the Church as Mother. She is its first member but more, she is a type of the Church, its locus. In an apocalyptic sense, Mary is the Church, the link between the Messianic motherhood of the Jesus of history, and the ecclesial motherhood of the Christ of faith. The entire mystery of divine life-giving is strangely and marvellously centred on her who is herself centred in the heart of the Trinity. Never Mary alone therefore, but Filiocentric Mary, Mary in communion with Christ, totally united with him who, proceeding eternally from the heavenly Father, emerges again and again into time and space from the depths of her virginal faith.

This is why the Book of Revelation presents her as constantly giving birth, constantly in labour, constantly in confrontation with the dragon waiting to consume her Child, the children of the New Israel.

A great portent appeared in heaven, a woman clothed with the sun, with the moon under her feet, and on her head a crown of twelve stars; she was with child and she cried out in her pangs of birth, in anguish for delivery. . . . And the dragon stood before the woman who was about to bear a child, that he might devour her child when she brought it forth. (12:1–2; 4)

The early Fathers had it that the labour pain Mary was spared at Bethlehem, she endured at Calvary. In the same mystical sense that pain has never ceased for Mary as Church. St Paul speaks of the whole creation in fact groaning in one great act of giving birth as it waits with eager longing for the revealing of the sons of God (Rom. 8:19). 'We know that the whole creation has been groaning in travail together until now; and not only the creation, but we ourselves, who have the first fruits of the Spirit, groan inwardly as we wait for adoption as sons, the redemption of our bodies' (Rom. 8:22–23). Because this anguish is the prelude to glory Paul rejoices 'in my sufferings for your sake, and in my flesh I complete what is lacking in Christ's afflictions for the sake of his body, that is, the church' (Col. 1:24).

What is lacking in Christ's affliction is its extension. It is not complete until every one of his members is brought to maturity. His passion therefore must continue to the end of time. Then his definitive triumph will be fully revealed. The Church as Mother, prefigured in Mary, not only bears the pain that children bring as they spring into existence. It endures the even greater anguish of standing by them as at Golgotha – sometimes just as powerless – as they struggle with themselves towards the fulness of life. In this it is helped by the personal intercession of Mary for, as Vatican II teaches, the 'motherhood of Mary in the order of grace continues uninterruptedly from the consent . . . which she sustained without wavering

beneath the cross, until the eternal fulfilment of all the elect'
(*Lumen gentium*, §62).

The two dimensions of her spiritual maternity – that of
intercession and that of participation in the Paschal Mystery –
are anticipated at the start of John's Gospel, at the marriage
feast of Cana. On the literal level her concern for the lack of
wine indicates the quality of her faith in Christ, in his ability
to supply what is needed. Her words, 'Do whatever he tells
you' (John 2:5), also indicate her evangelical role of inspiring
faith in others. The fact that Jesus responds to her request
despite his apparent unreadiness ('O woman, what have you
to do with me?' – 2:4), alerts us to her future sphere of
influence as one who has access to the heart of Christ.

On the level of signs, since the wedding feast is a figure
of the eschatological banquet celebrated in sacrament at the
Eucharist which flows from Christ's heart on the cross, her
intervention is to be seen as a petition for grace. What she
asks for she will receive. It will cost her more than Abraham
was asked to pay: the price of her Son. Nevertheless she will
pay it because it is the price that God himself must pay since
her Son is his Son too.

Realising this, the community of the Disciple who took her
to his home as Mother of the Church, station her at the Fourth
Gospel's beginning and its end. These two points locate her
proper place in the plan of salvation. When she appears a third
time in the Johannine corpus (Rev. 12), it will be clothed with
the sun and the moon and the stars, a tribute to her cosmic
Motherhood; for in sharing the sufferings of Christ and the
Church, she reigns forever with him who is King of the
Universe.

This universal matriarchy clearly identifies Mary as the new
Eve. Not surprisingly the ravenous beast that confronts her in

the Apocalypse is no less than 'that ancient serpent, who is called the Devil or Satan, the deceiver of the whole world' (12:9). Eden has been re-staged, freedom and grace re-tested. But even now the outcome is decided, the victory won. Obedience and faith have been given by the Woman to God; Calvary has occurred; a new Adam and Eve have reversed the tragedy of the original couple. Satan is too late, for the saving mystery has already been accomplished in silence before he has had time even to know his defeat.

In the sub-apostolic age St Ignatius of Antioch gave a prominent place to this theme in his writing. His Letter to the Ephesians, for example, provided a classic expression of the idea that was much prized by the later patristic writers: 'Mary's virginity was hidden from the prince of this world; so was her child-bearing, and so was the death of the Lord. All these three trumpet-tongued secrets were brought to pass in the deep silence of God' (§19).

This early Christian comment, so close to the written Gospels and addressed to the city where (if legend is true) the Virgin Mother and John went to live, where the cult of the pagan mother-goddess, Diana (Artemis), once flourished, and where the fifth-century Church in Council would proclaim Mary *Theotokos* (Mother of God), is enlightening. It explains Mary's absence of speech at the cross: her quiet assent to the will of the Father confounds the idle chatter of Eve to the serpent. It explains too the silence of God in the face of human suffering: the hidden reserves of his wisdom and power are more than humankind can fathom for all man's reflection on the mystery of good and evil.

Mary's significance as the new Eve is underscored by the attachment of the title 'Woman' to her in every text where she appears in the Johannine corpus. This was how the old Eve was known before she received a personal name. To attribute it now to Mary is to evoke the text in Genesis of the Fall and to show by contrast how the knot of sin tied by man's first help-mate was untied with the help of his second.

Jesus' specification of her gender at Calvary was very deliberate. It was not the way a son addressed his mother and has no precedent in scripture. The Gospel, in reporting it, means us to see here a soteriological sign. As Christ consciously offers up his life to destroy the reign of Satan, equally he solicits the assent of Womanhood, the means by which Satan gained access to Adam. If justice demands that by man shall man's fault be rectified, full justice demands that woman be included in the act of expiation. As Eve, attracted by the fruit of a tree, ruptured the first covenant with the Lord God, so Mary, eating the bitter fruit of the cross, announces the new covenant. Sinful woman with sinful man brought forth a sinful race; new woman, full of grace, with God-made-man brings forth a holy people. The first man called his woman 'Mother of all who live', though she was Mother of all who die. The second Man calls his Mother 'Woman', because all whom she conceives will live forever.

The cross was the second occasion when Jesus addressed his Mother thus. Cana was the other. 'O woman, what have you to do with me?' (John 2:4). The question is full of import. It is theological as well as rhetorical, challenging and provocative. Coming at the start of the Gospel, it invites discussion, arouses hope. Because the nuptials are prelude to the death at Golgotha, Mary's role at Cana prepares us for her role at Calvary. The repetition of 'Woman' draws the two scenes together, showing not only the intrinsic relationship between them in terms of Jesus' messianism, but also the consistency of the Virgin's mission in helping him accomplish it.

At Cana therefore, the use of 'Woman' dares the sinful world to take heart. Referring covertly to Eden (too tragic to spell out overtly), it confirms the joyful drift of John's theme, 'And the Word became flesh' (1:14); confirms the promise from Eden of a Woman's seed to crush the serpent's head. Those who knew the text and looked at Mary, who heard what Jesus called her and watched how she responded, would have understood as the Beloved Disciple understood without another word being said.

'What have you to do with me? My hour has not yet come.' In John, 'the hour' means the time of Christ's passion, the moment of glory. It is fixed and appointed in the divine plan. When it comes Mary will be needed. Then she will have much to do with Christ. At the wedding banquet his words are a speech from heart to heart. Not yet comprehended by all present, they would have said everything to her who pondered these things in her mind and treasured them in her breast. She does not ask for explanation but readies herself for action. Like the advice she gives to those around her, she too will 'do whatever he tells'. It is as woman she will do it: as spouse to his Spirit, as mother to the Son himself, as daughter to his Father. All things to God to whom she surrenders her entire femininity, to redeem the name of Woman that Eve betrayed.

From Genesis to Apocalypse the figure of a Woman central to God's plan has spanned the course of salvation history with her silent, enigmatic presence. At Calvary she now becomes visible. Present from the start of man's story in prophecy, a vine of encouragement, she is still there at its projected end, a vision of harvest. Opening and closing the Biblical narrative of God's victory over evil – as she opens and closes the Gospel's account of Christ's kingship – she is herself the sign and fruit of God's glorious achievement.

As the new Adam falls into the exhausted sleep of suffering and triumph, the Woman who materialises at his side, the new Mary, is no longer the Virgin of Nazareth that was. Her soul scraped from the bone that the lance laid bare, her being re-shaped by the tearing of his flesh, she is totally God's creation. There is no will left in her but his. She is, of all creatures, alone a fitting partner for the Man; but like Eve before her she must wait for him to wake and acknowledge her, the Church, as bone of his bone, flesh of his flesh, and worthy once more of Paradise.

Until then she goes on enduring what he has ceased to feel: the terrible Day of the Lord when the very universe shudders for gladness, the stars tumble from heaven, and the sun's light diminishes against the splendour of the radiant Lamb slain for his royal bride.

First Mother of the Beloved Son, then Mother of the Beloved Disciple, and now Mother of all who assemble at the foot of the cross, her threefold maternity sacramentalises the maternal love of the invisible Father. What the world cannot see of his consuming fire, she shows. Her human pity, so heavy with pain, so totally accepting, locates his devastating pity for his creation. What men never would have believed, she holds out for them to look on: the pale, limp corpse of her Child not yet cold, who dared to measure Love's dreadful love for his Beloved People: 'O righteous Father, [now] may the world know that you have loved them even as you have loved me' (John 17:25, 23).

Throughout the silent universe no living voice was raised to contradict the dead.

The Burial

ACCORDING TO ALL THE Gospel accounts Jesus' funeral was just as brutal as his death. Each tells of the sordid haste to get rid of the body before sundown when the sabbath begins. The Authorities wanted it out of sight, hidden away, for – as John explains – that particular sabbath 'was a high day' (19:31), their Passover. A corpse was an objectionable thing, unclean. It would not be fitting to leave it hanging in public on the Jewish Feast of feasts.

There was no time therefore for mourning rites. No gathering of sympathisers as at Lazarus' funeral (John 11:19), no customary laying out of the remains after washing as at Tabitha's wake (Acts 9:37), no opportunity to prepare spices and ointments as a last service and mark of respect for the dead (Luke 23:56; Mark 16:1).

Worst of all – this from the Johannine account again – was the mutilation of the corpse in front of the mourners. Not content with humiliating him in the passion, the militia had to desecrate his remains before they let Jesus go. The callousness and nonchalance of the act make it especially horrific.

The whole event is horrific. It needs no colouring from the sacred writers to make it worse. Their straight reporting of facts says it all. The indignity accorded to the dead man is nothing short of remarkable. No civilised society disposes of its deceased – including those condemned to capital punishment – without some measure of decorum. For Jesus there was none.

That he was a Jew in his own country makes his treatment the more shocking. He was after all one of the Chosen People. Mosaic law was meant to protect their dignity, to enhance it. Jewish codes of decency towards common humanity were still more binding towards fellow Israelites. Yet in death Jesus is denied the common decency that even his humanity deserves; instead his corpse is abused like a carcass, dismissed like offal by Roman and Hebrew officials together.

In Mark-Matthew the burial itself is particularly stark. A linen shroud, a hewn tomb, a stone rolled against the door, and the funeral is over. Only the Marcan Appendix (chapter 16), the later reconstruction of the Gospel's lost ending, mentions the bringing of spices on the Sunday morning. Matthew was not even thinking of such details. In his account the tomb belonged to 'a rich man from Arimathea, named Joseph' (27:57, 60). The phraseology calls to mind once again the Fourth Song of the Suffering Servant in the prophet Isaiah, the bitter text that guided his telling of the passion:

> He was cut off out of the land of the living. . . .
> And they made his grave with the wicked
> and with a rich man in his death,
> although he had done no violence.

(Isa. 53:9)

Mark's narrative is the shortest possible. Matthew pauses only to add that the moment the body was interred Joseph of Arimathea 'departed', leaving two of the women 'sitting there opposite the sepulchre' (27:60–61). It was no place for the rich or the squeamish. And to note, for the record, the offensive security arrangements by the cold and determined Pharisees to have the grave guarded by a corps of foreign soldiers.

Luke's treatment of the story is gentler, in keeping with his portrait of the forgiving, gentle Saviour. Joseph of Arimathea, for example, is sympathetically sketched. He was 'a good and righteous man'; he 'had not consented to their purpose and deed'; he did not have to summon up courage (as in Mark) to ask Pilate for the body; he was one 'looking for the kingdom of God' (Luke 23:50–52). The women at the scene soften the harshness; they lend a touch of domestic order to the chaos; the account ends with their returning to prepare the spices and ointments which have not been forgotten (23:55–56). If the tender-hearted doctor's tale is short, one feels it is because he has resurrection in mind and wishes not to make more of the death than Jesus himself would make.

Thus without omitting the inhumane treatment of Christ, Luke manages to make it the backdrop against which the compassionate spirit of Jesus still hovers. Projected positively on to others through Luke's optimism, this spirit – so characteristic of his Gospel – focuses on the good that is done by all who helped at this difficult time. Already the pathos of Good Friday is giving way to something wonderful about to happen.

In John's Gospel it already has. For all the venom of the Jews, Christ's going into the tomb is simply a laying-down to rest. The attentive care lavished on his body suggests an expectation of his awaking. It implies that his dignity remains unimpaired despite the marks in his hands, feet and side. It seems to assume a destiny for this corpse other than corruption.

Not only is Jesus' body embalmed like that of a king, but the spices are named: 'a mixture of aloes and myrrh' (19:39). It evokes a verse in the messianic Psalms from the love song composed for a royal wedding, addressed to the bridegroom:

> God, your God, has anointed you
> with the oil of gladness, above all your rivals;
> myrrh and aloes waft from your robes.

(Ps. 44/45. JB)

Moreover the mixture is not mean. It is 'about a hundred pounds' weight' (19:39). An extravagant profusion of lavish opulence that outdoes the earlier anointing in John when Mary of Bethany prepared him in anticipation of this day with balsam. 'Mary took a pound of costly ointment of pure nard (worth a year's salary) and anointed the feet of Jesus . . . and the house was filled with fragrance' (12:3). Now, as then, the action is a faith-proclamation of his Messiahship. Indeed the anointing at the tomb is a hundred times more glorious, more weighty than before, since the cause of their believing lies prostrate before their eyes. The aromatic odour of this sacrifice will not just fill a house; it will break through the walls of the grave and fill the entire cosmos.

Here the corpse is not simply 'wrapped in a linen cloth' as in the synoptics. Rather 'they took the body of Jesus, and bound it in linen cloths with the spices, as is the burial custom of the Jews' (19:40). Full protocol is observed, as is fitting for the King of the Jews. But more, the language connotes the tender care with which a new-born child is dressed. One cannot help but think of Luke's infancy narrative (of all the synoptics he was always most like John), when the Virgin Mary 'gave birth to her first-born son and wrapped him in swaddling cloths, and laid him in a manger' (Luke 2:7). As at his birth so at his burial. While there may be no room in the inn, no room in Israel's heart for him, there are those who will lift him and clothe him and lay him gently to rest.

And just as once he entered the virginal womb, so now he enters a virginal tomb 'where no one had ever been laid' (John 19:41). Mary housed him safely during gestation while he was an unborn child; now the sepulchre becomes his mother, pregnant with the unborn Resurrection.

'In the place where he was crucified there was a garden, and in the garden a new tomb. . . . So as the tomb was close at hand, they laid Jesus there' (John 19:41–42). The garden, twice referred to, is the new Eden. The story of salvation has turned full circle. We are back to the point where it all began and from where the new start has already begun. Once again Adam sleeps. When he wakes he will not be driven out like before by the flaming sword of the cherubim 'which turned every way, to guard the way to the tree of life' (Gen. 3:24). For the fruit of the tree of life has been consumed, and that life will no longer be cursed by the intrusion of death.

No mention is made of the stone that was rolled in front of Jesus' tomb. It was there but John considers it irrelevant. Soon no grave will require a capping stone. Death's days are numbered. In the kingdom that Jesus has won the very concept will be unknown.

It is now Holy Saturday, the seventh day. The world is quiet, the whole universe hushed. The King sleeps; Adam slumbers; it is God's sabbath rest. To the psalmist of old such stillness was anathema. It inspired him with panic and despair. His people suffered under constant oppression while God seemed unaware. From within and without Israel laboured under injustice and God seemed to be in a coma, indifferent when they needed him most.

Awake, O Lord, why do you sleep?
Arise, do not reject us forever!. . . .
For we are brought down low to the dust;
our body lies prostrate on the earth.
Stand up and come to our help.

(Ps. 43/44)

From the depths of the rocky tomb the words of the psalm echo back. They are now the words of God himself. It is he who is brought down low to the dust, God's body that lies prostrate on the earth, the Son of God who sleeps the sleep of the dead, crucified by the injustices under which Israel has laboured so long. Never again can it be said that the Father does not care. Nor that he has rejected his children. If God is silent when his people are in pain, it is but the silence of one who suffers with them and for them in the flesh of the Beloved Son. Taking their poverty on himself, he raises them up as he himself will arise in order to shepherd them lovingly home to the house of his Beloved Father.

'For the poor who are oppressed and the needy who groan
I myself will arise', says the Lord.
'I will grant them the salvation for which they thirst.'

(Ps. 11/12)

The moribund sun is setting in the west. Already the paschal fires of Christendom are burning. When the morning sun rises again in the east it will bring the Light that shines forever.